Emotional and Narcissistic Abuse

The Complete Survival Guide to Understanding Narcissism, Escaping the Narcissist in a Toxic Relationship Forever, and Your Road to Recovery

J. Vandeweghe

Table of Contents

FREE AUDIOBOOK

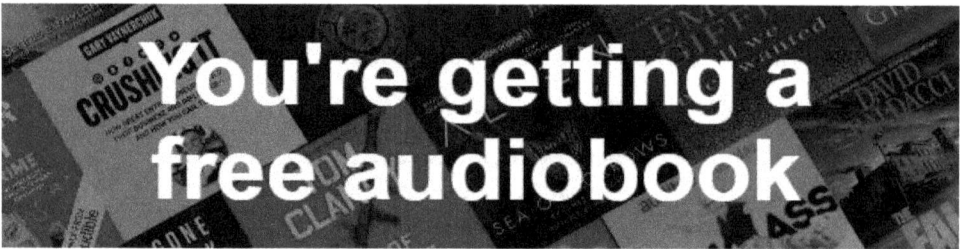

Feel like listening instead?

Save yourself $14.95 and click the link below to get the Audiobook Edition for FREE

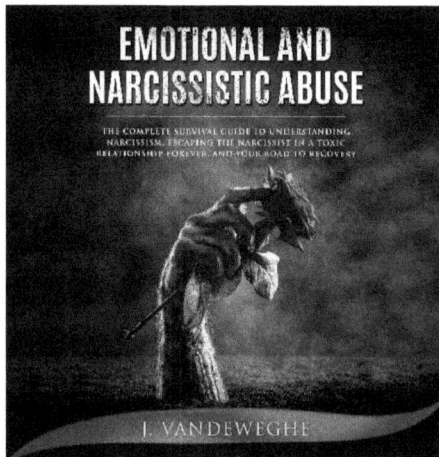

For US:
http://bit.ly/Narc_FreeAudiobook_US

For UK:
http://bit.ly/Narc_FreeAudiobook_UK

Please note: Must be a new member to Audible

Free E-book and Newsletter

PERSEVERING THROUGH 'NO-CONTACT' HANDBOOK

Click the link below to sign up to the newsletter and receive a free Handbook on Persevering Through 'No-Contact.' There is some helpful advice in there and a great source to turn to when you in moments of struggle.

http://bit.ly/No-Contact-Handbook

Introduction

Thank you for purchasing *"Emotional and Narcissistic Abuse: The Complete Survival Guide to Understanding Narcissism, Escaping the Narcissist in a Toxic Relationship Forever, and Your Road to Recovery."*

If you are reading this book, it is likely because you are seeking support for leaving from an abusive, narcissistic relationship. Or want to find ways to heal. This book has been written to inform you on narcissism, narcissistic personality disorder, the cycles of abuse, the symptoms of the relationship, the damage to the victim, and how you can safely escape and heal from a narcissistic relationship.

While this book goes into depth on all of the information you need to know regarding narcissism and the abusive relationships you may endure with a narcissistic partner, it is important to understand that this book does not substitute a professional therapist. Abusive relationships can be tricky and, as you will learn, the depth of the trauma can be deep in these types of relationships. Having access to a professionally trained therapist can be vital in helping you heal from everything you go through, including understanding what happened and healing from it all.

That being said, this book will provide you with great value and insight on everything you are going through and what you need to do next. If you are still in the relationship, this will support you in the process of beginning to demystify everything that has been going on and recognizing the reality of what you are experiencing. As you will learn, this is an essential part of breaking free from the relationship and healing.

I hope that this book finds you well and safe and that everything within these pages supports you in understanding more about your relationship. I also hope it helps you to safely leave your relationship so that you can move on to the healing process and eventually resume a happy, healthy lifestyle. Remember, it is never your fault.

Chapter 1: A Narcissistic Love Story

This is the story of a narcissist and his (or her) victim. This is the story that every narcissistic abuse victim will recognize and understand. It is a painful truth of the life of someone who is in love with a narcissist. For the purpose of this story, the narcissist has been referred to as a male. It should be noted that NOT all narcissists are male.

"You recall the beginning when it was so sweet and so pure. It began simply: with love and tenderness. The chemistry was insanely powerful, so much so that you felt like you had known this person for life. It was effortless. Whenever you were with him, you felt higher and higher. It was a match made in heaven, or so you thought.

Every conversation you shared, every text you sent, felt so right. He made you feel like the only person in the world – like you were his one true love. Like this would have a fairytale ending. This was going to be your happy ending, and you were ready for your Prince Charming to whisk you away on his white horse. Until you realized Prince Charming was not so charming and his horse was nowhere to be found.

It was not too long before you began to see the mask slip. The face he carefully curated just for his entertainment, to reel you in, began to fall off. It started slowly, a single incident amidst the perfect relationship. Everything else was so right that you managed to justify these behaviors. After all, he helped you do it, didn't he? He told you it was work, or you did something to upset him. He was entirely justified in his actions. He was still your perfect Prince Charming.

Everything went back to normal until it happened again. This time his rage grew stronger, more powerful. He carefully crafted together a fabric of falsehoods. He used the worst miseries from your past and the most intense insecurities from your present to justify his behavior. It's your fault for upsetting him, or not trusting him. You should have known better. What were you thinking?

Slowly, he introduces new ways to torment you. More people enter the scene, consistently tearing away from your Prince Charming relationship. He praises them and shames you. Winning is his favorite pass-time, and when he sees you squirm, he knows he is winning this game.

Your reality begins to turn into a falsehood that he creates for you. You grow more and more doubtful of your inner voice, allowing you to justify his behavior further. You knew he didn't like that, why did you do it anyway? His actions are your fault. You did this. Every strength you have becomes a flaw, every talent you have is a travesty, and all of your compassion is just you being naïve. He takes over your reality, stripping away your identity, memory, and self-esteem. Rapidly, his weaknesses are your weaknesses, and he projects every inch of his reality unto you. Your mind drips his stories, and you hungrily eat them up. Your reality is no longer your own. It is his now. He has taken over.

The narcissist does not believe in true love until the love becomes addicting. Until it becomes a game of give-and-take. One where he gives the abuse and takes your self-confidence, self-worth, and identity away completely. One where he gives you poison and takes away the real antidote.

You begin to question yourself and everything he has done. You can feel the cruelty, but you start to wonder if it was really meant to be cruel or not. Maybe it was a mistake? Perhaps he did not realize what he was doing? Your once carefree, lighthearted and loving spirit fades as you begin to feel insecure and oversensitive. You wonder if you are crazy. You question everything your insides tell you. Is this real? Is any of this real?

As you crumble and find yourself struggling to decipher reality from this falsehood, he continues to hide his intentions and layer on the abuse. He showers you with gentle love and sprinkles you with condescending contempt. You can never decide what is what. You are continually being poisoned and then remedied, over and over and over again.

Each time the love is taken away, and you are left in the midst of the cruelty, you find yourself reeling. Withdrawal from this drug is painful, and you so desperately need your next fix. Your addiction validates his destruction. This is how he knows he is winning the game. He has you right where he wants you.

The abuse accelerates to the point that you are now admitting defeat toward it all on a daily basis. He becomes meaner and meaner, testing you to see how far he can take it. Will you take it? He accelerates from harsh words and sarcastic jabs to condescending put-downs and full-out attacks. The entire relationship is a power play, and he refuses to let you win this battle for dominance. Instead, he makes you feel like you are winning from time to time, only so he can strike you down once more.

Each time you default to defeat faster, he rips you apart further. The wounds layer upon you, cutting away at who you are and locking you within his mental prison. He abuses you while forcing you to doubt the abuse, leading you to believe there is no abuse genuinely happening in this relationship. Your quiet inner voice screams out for protection, but the voice he has grown within you silences it and pushes you to believe him and hold on to the false reality of who this man really is.

The fairy tale has ended, but you no longer have the strength or ability to walk away. You are left facing the nightmare. This is no longer a game that he (or she) needs to win. This is a nightmare that you need to awaken from. Perhaps you will awaken from it over and over, awaiting the opportunity for you to realize that you are no longer dreaming and this is all very real.

In this love story, the happy ending is not one of romance and forever-after. This happy ending lies in you realizing Prince Charming never existed, and this was all a twisted game of narcissist-and-mouse."

Chapter 2: The Real Narcissist

The casual tossing-around of the word "narcissist" has led many people to falsely believe that a narcissist is simply someone who has an inflated sense of confidence and perhaps a slightly inflated ego, too. Unfortunately, the dictionary reinforces this belief with its description of a narcissist, stating that they are "a person who has an excessive interest in or admiration of themselves." This is more likely to be the definition of someone who is arrogant and not someone who is narcissistic. The reality of a narcissist is much darker than that.

Narcissists do tend to think incredibly highly of themselves, but the reality of who they are and what they do is extremely intricate and well-played. Narcissism is an intricate, well-constructed series of traits wrapped up in one mental illness that is extremely damaging to all who cross the paths of a narcissist, especially their lovers.

Some people are known to possess narcissistic-like qualities, but this is entirely different from what a true narcissist is. A true narcissist is a master at lying, phenomenal at deception, and incredibly talented at curating codependent victims. They are powerful. Because a narcissist is generally slow and consistent in their approach, they are masters at tearing down other people to the point that the other person develops an addiction to the narcissist. The narcissist is not just in love with getting attention; they are completely addicted to it. That is the basis for their entire mental illness. It is what drives them and what results in them masterfully playing out all of their puppeteering behaviors.

Who is a Narcissist?

If you ask someone who a narcissist is, most people will describe an arrogant, entitled, privileged male. This is the persona that has been promoted as "narcissist" in most people's lives. However, the reality is that narcissists are not quite as defined as that. A narcissist can truly be anyone. There is no preferred gender, age, or race that narcissism chooses. Instead, anyone can be a narcissist.

In the United States, it is estimated that 1 in every 25 people is a sociopath. As you will learn about later in this chapter, sociopaths are those who are at the top end of the spectrum that also contains psychopaths and narcissists. The number of narcissistic individuals living in modern America is surprisingly large. The majority of us come across at least one in our lives that impacts us in some way. For some of us, that impact is significant. For others, they recognize the behavior to be negative and walk away.

Rather than looking at the demographics of "who" a narcissist is, it is easier to identify one by their traits. The list of characteristics that a narcissist has that identifies their narcissistic behaviors is reasonably straightforward and is the easiest way to determine a narcissist. Attempting to use statistical evidence around their demographic will not result in an accurate finding.

What are the Traits of a Narcissist?

Paying attention to the traits of an individual is the easiest way to identify whether or not someone is a narcissist. If you want to identify one, pay attention to the list of traits below and take a moment to consider if the person you are questioning possesses these traits. This will support you in understanding if they truly are a narcissist.

People with narcissistic personality disorder possess these traits:

A Complete Lack of Empathy
First and foremost, someone who is narcissistic possesses a complete lack of empathy. Those with a narcissistic personality disorder do not simply lack empathy; they are mentally incapable of experiencing it. This results in them being incapable of identifying the emotions or feelings of others and taking them into account.

Due to a lack of empathy, people who are narcissistic will struggle to behave in a way that shows any compassion toward other humans. They are incapable of understanding how their actions impact others, and as a result, they are known to regularly behave in a way that is mentally damaging to others. This is how they build on their abuse without showing any signs of feeling remorseful for it: because they truly cannot feel remorse. It can be very toxic and draining to be around someone who has so sign of empathy nor takes responsibility for their actions.

Grandiose Sense of Self-Importance

People who are narcissistic are known to have an elated sense of self-importance. They will often lie about their achievements to make them sound better than they are. They also lie about their talents so that people will believe they are more capable than they actually are. A narcissist does not just want to be recognized and superior and better, they expect to be. Regardless of what their actual achievements are, even if they are incredibly few or irrelevant, they expect to be seen as the superior person. No matter what, a narcissist wants to be seen as better than everyone else they meet.

Fantasizes About Unlimited Power or Success

Narcissistic people are obsessed with their fantasies about unlimited power and success. They like to fantasize about being better than everyone else in every way possible, from their looks to their life. They want to be the best at activities, in relationships, in their family, at work, and in virtually every area of their life. They will do everything they can to make it appear as though they have the best life possible and that it is better than anyone else's. This enables narcissists to have an unrealistic belief of what their life truly is, which often provides a strong basis for how they are able to deceive other people into believing their fantasy reality versus the actual reality.

Believe They are "Special"

Individuals who are narcissistic have a belief that they are "special" in some way. This promotes their inner belief that they are superior to others and why they act so entitled. They believe that they are only capable of being understood by other "special" people, who are typically only those of high-status. In fact, many believe they should only associate with people of high-status or institutions of high-status and often think that they are above everyone else. This belief can be seen in their arrogant behaviors, their attitude toward other people, and the way that they talk themselves up in groups.

Addicted to Attention

The narcissist's addiction to attention is the driving force behind everything that they do. Narcissists do not just crave attention; they *need* it. This is why they will lie about everything, fantasize about massive success and power, and otherwise focus on things that will earn them some attention including drama. They may be particularly focused on grooming and maintaining a very poised outward image (their mask, or false-self: see Chapter 5). This is how they are able to draw in all of the attention they crave from other people.

Because of their need for attention, narcissists become abusive. Their carefully crafted abuse cycle enables them to cause other people to become codependent, resulting in these other people not having a sense of self-worth or identity. Then, they are pressured to see this individual as the "godly" aspect of their lives. The codependent will look to the narcissist for validation, approval, and acceptance. The narcissist will offer increments of validation, approval, and acceptances in dosages that become increasingly smaller over time. At first, their withholding of love and kindness only happens every once in a while. Eventually, it happens daily.

Is Envious or Believes Others Are Envious

Narcissists tend to go one or both ways with envy. They either tend to be chronically envious of everyone else which further drives their need for attention, or they believe that everyone else is envious of them. Most narcissists are both to a degree.

When they are envious of others, the narcissist will rarely say anything. Instead, they will begin to lie and exploit others, even more, to make it appear as though they are not envious and have nothing to be envious about. Remember, a narcissist does not only want to be the best in the room, but they truly believe they *are* at all times. They will say anything they need to say to ensure that everyone else believes this mask and regards them as the best, even if that includes lying, manipulating people, exploiting others, and otherwise being abusive to the people they know and, in many cases, do not know.

When they believe others are envious of them, this feeds into their need for attention. They feel good – like they are winning at their game.

They want other people to be envious of them because this is how people feel toward people who are "better." At least, that is what the narcissist believes. The narcissist will say and do anything it takes to ensure they are better than the others, even if they really are not, just so that the other people in the room become envious of them. This supports their need for attention and thus becomes one of their favorite tools for satisfying the addiction.

Arrogant Behavior or Attitude
Despite arrogance itself not being the measure of a narcissist, most narcissists are arrogant. This means that not all arrogant people are narcissists, but all narcissists are arrogant. This arrogant behavior and attitude supports them in promoting themselves as the best person in the room. It allows them to portray a higher degree of confidence then they actually possess, allowing them to appear "special" and better than others.

When a narcissist is arrogant, they are the maximum degree of arrogant they can possibly be. They are not just slightly arrogant or walking around with a somewhat inflated ego and sense of self-confidence. People with narcissistic personality disorder take arrogance to the next level. They are extremely inflated in their confidence and ego about absolutely everything. This is a tool they use to appear better, and they use it to the maximum degree.

Compulsive Liars
Narcissists are compulsive liars. As such, they are also experts at manipulating other people. Narcissists will expertly create a web of lies that support them in creating their desired reality and bringing other people into it. If they are ever caught in a lie, they will masterfully create more lies to cover up the lies that they have already told. In this process, they are not worried about who they hurt or who they blame through their lies. Their only concern is in ensuring that they are protected and that they come out looking like the winner in one way or another.

When a narcissist is not outright lying, they will purposefully leave out important pieces of information. Or, they will stonewall the victim by refusing to answer any questions or by providing evasive answers to the questions being asked. This is another way of them creating a blameless crime where they can easily spin it around to look like it was someone else's fault for not asking for the information outright, even though they knew that the chances of the other person thinking to ask would be slim. This is how they ensure that even when they are lying, they cannot be blamed for their lies. If anything, you can be blamed for not pressing for more information.

No matter how much you continue digging to discover what the full truth is or attempting to untangle their lies, you will never get to the real truth. They will continue dancing around the situation until you are so exhausted that you stop. If you do not exhaust before finally reaching their breaking point, you will be so tired from chasing that you are no longer able to fight or stand up for yourself, thus meaning you are still a victim of the lie even if you finally get to the truth. Either way, the narcissist wins.

Openly Exploits Victims on Social Media
A narcissist has a deep addiction to exploiting their victims. These days, social media has given them the power to exploit, even more, resulting in their victims suffering even further. There are at least five major ways that narcissists will take advantage of social media to exploit you, should they so desire.

The first way is by using social media to enhance further their favorite abuse tool of "triangulation," which you will learn about in greater depth in Chapter 7. In essence, they will bring another person into the mixture and embarrass you by giving more attention to the other person then is typically reasonable or acceptable for a relationship. This may lead to you believing they are cheating because they share pictures of them with this other person, or they comment more on their photos than they do on yours, thus making it clearly visible that this other person is getting more attention than you do. Then, when you attempt to point this act out, they will blame you for overreacting or reading something into it when they claim that nothing is actually happening.

They will also use social media as a way to spy on you. Narcissists will often follow you on social media and pay attention to your goings on online to see what you are doing and see anything that they could use against you. This helps them learn more about what you like, what you are interested in, how you speak to your friends, and otherwise. Later, they will use this information in their love-bombing stage where they attract your attention and get you to fall in love with them. Then, they will use this exact same information to abuse you by calling you names or ridiculing you for your various interests and the things you post or share.

Not only will a narcissist spy on you during the relationship and use the information against you, but they will also use it after the relationship ends as a way to stalk and harass you. If you have ever tried to leave the relationship in the past, you can likely recall them stalking everything you are doing and regularly messaging you and trying to get in touch with you so that they could attempt to lure you back into the relationship. This is done in a way that is enough to feel like a clear violation but is typically not done so much so that it violates harassment laws enough to result in any type of persecution.

They will also use social media as a way to embellish their grandiose sense of self. They will post only images that they feel boosts their popularity and social status as a way to feed their constant need for attention. Then, when they actually get likes, they will use this as a way to make others look lesser to them because they are not getting as much attention. Therefore, they can make it look like the other person is not cared about or likable. If you are in a relationship with these people, they will likely use you as a way to increase their popularity. For example, they may post provocative pictures of you or ones that make you look bad in some way but can be twisted to make them look good. This makes you look like the lesser person in the relationship and, as a result of their manipulation, makes them look like the good person even though they are posting pictures without your consent that show you off in a bad, uncomfortable, or inappropriate way. Not only does this feed their need to look good, but it can also further isolate you from others in your life because it may cause those you are close with to begin thinking less of you and believing that you are engaging in negative behavior, rather than the true fact which is that the person you were with exploited you and treated you abusively.

Lastly, social media provides an excellent platform for narcissists to bully and taunt other people. Online, narcissists take pleasure in provoking people to begin engaging in an argument but spin the entire thing to make it look like it is the other persons' fault. They tend to be extremely cruel and violent, often threatening peoples' physical wellbeing or livelihood altogether.

Talks Behind People's Backs

Social media is not the only place where a narcissist will exploit their victims. Narcissists also like to talk behind people's backs when they are not around as a way to make them look better and create drama. One of the most frustrating things about this is that it can take an awfully long time before you realize this is happening. The narcissist is incredibly smart and tactical when it comes to these games. When you do realize, it becomes very painful and challenging to accept, especially when these accusations remarks about you are completely false. In virtually every scenario where you are not around, and the narcissist sees an opportunity to use you to increase their sense of self, and harm your social image, they will. Typically, this talk will be degrading and will result in you being made out to sound like you are worthless, incapable and despised while the narcissist appears to always come out as the hero in the story. To them, it is a way of making themselves look great. For you, it can feel like they are making you out to sound like some form of an incompetent fool.

Energy Vampires

Because of their compulsive lying, the constant need for attention, addiction to drama and their grandiose sense of self, narcissists are one of the highest forms of the energy vampire. They require a lot of time and attention from other people, often resulting in them willing to go to extreme lengths to get it. If you are in a relationship with them, they will naturally rely on you to be their main source of energy. When things become stagnant, the narcissist loves to create completely false accusations and situations to put you on the back foot and defend yourself. The narcissist loves creating drama and fights as a way to suck the energy out of you and make you work harder for their love and approval. As such, you may find yourself feeling constantly drained and exhausted by them. They will leach onto your energy until they can no longer do so because you are exhausted and have no energy left to give.

Once they see you reach this weakened state, they will initiate the part of their abuse cycle where they begin to decimate your sense of self-esteem and self-confidence. This will drive you to a breaking point where you can no longer handle their abuse. Then, when you are just about ready to give up and find your freedom or peace, they come back with their love-bombing and try to refuel your energy tank. This result's in a deep battle between you and them where you long to get away and feel free once again, but their energy vampire traits result's in a vicious roller-coaster ride.

High Sex Drive

Energy is transferred in large amounts through sexual acts. For this reason, many narcissists have an incredibly high sex drive. They always want to have sex with you, exploit you during sex, and be made to feel like they are the "dominant" one during their sex with you. This is because they get a lot of energy out of this experience. It also is a great way for them to amplify the roller-coaster-like abuse-cycle. If they have been super-abusive to you lately and feel you slipping away from their web, they may try to love-bomb you with attention and sex. Because they are having sex with you, they will often make it seem like it will be a mutually enjoyable experience. That is until it begins. Once you start having sex with them, most of the time they generally become selfish lovers and will only engage in the forms of sex that they want. If they do happen to give in to what you want, you can almost always guarantee that it will come back on you later as a situation where "I let you ____, so you owe me!" or "I did ____ which is proof of how much I love you!" type statements are used. This is a way to twist it to seem like they are generous and considerate of your feelings, but later they use this generosity as a way to get their own needs met and send yours down once again.

Inability to Feel Guilt or Remorse

As a result of their lack of empathy, narcissists have a complete inability to feel guilty or remorseful for anything that they have done. They are literally incapable, meaning that no matter what you do or say they will never truly feel bad for their actions. However, this is not always apparent at first glance. In many instances, when it serves them, narcissists will *mimic* guilt or remorse as a way to make it appear as though they are genuinely sorry for what they have done or that they genuinely feel bad for creating chaos or destruction in your life in one way or another. This, however, is absolutely never a real sense of guilt or remorse. Instead, it is their way of getting you to believe that they did not have any ill intentions, thus allowing them to jump back on track to serve their own needs quickly. In some cases, they realize that arguing with you over their mistakes may take away too much from their end goal: to win. So, they will use their fake remorse as a way to avoid the hassle and get to where they want to be even faster. Plus, they can use this as "evidence" that they do feel bad when they hurt you, thus giving them the opportunity to make you sound crazy for believing that they always hurt you intentionally and without any concern. This keeps you roped in and believing their lies for as long as possible. Eventually, there will come a time where it is clearly evident that they are incapable of feeling remorseful or guilty for their actions. It is a painful truth to face and can be extremely difficult to comprehend how someone can be so cruel and numb. By this time, it is usually too late and you are deeply in the abuse cycle.

Inability to Apologize or Admit Wrong-doing
One thing that you can guarantee about a narcissist is that they will never admit to being wrong. Narcissists do not, under any circumstances, apologize for their behavior or actions. They absolutely never will. If they do, you must never believe that this is a true admission of their mistake. Instead, they are using it as a bargaining chip to twist it around and make it sound like they made a mistake either because they were forced to (which transfers the blame away from them) or because it was supportive of the bigger picture (which in the end only feeds their needs and ego). The other time they will apologize is when you have done absolutely everything in your power to get them to apologize, and they have effectively sucked the life out of you, so they throw you a bone. But you can be absolutely sure there will be no truth or meaning to their apology. There is virtually never a sincere admission of a mistake from a narcissist. Why would they apologize to you when they don't even feel any sense of guilt or remorse for what they have done? Instead, they are more likely to lie and create another false sense of reality. Be aware of this.

Experts at Playing the Victim

Another trait narcissists carry as a result of being masters at manipulating is their ability to "turn the tables" and project onto others. Narcissists love to twist the switch around so that it seems like *you* were actually the one to do something that *they* did. For example, say you are in the middle of an argument, and a narcissist begins calling you names and bullying you. If you were to later in the argument point this out and call them out on it, the narcissist would start projecting, saying that you were the one bullying them and anything they said was only a means of defending themselves against your bullying. This means that they can expertly become the victim of any situation and make you out to be the attacker. Because you are not the one playing the head games, but instead you are the real victim, what can end up happening is two situations.

1. You feel the guilt and remorse that they are incapable of feeling. You will likely begin questioning your own actions and looking to verify what they have said. If they point out any specific evidence, you will immediately start feeling bad and trying to make up for what you have said or done, even though you likely never announced or did it with any malicious intent. As a result, they end up with the upper hand, and you are left apologizing to them and trying to make up for what you supposedly did when in reality they are the ones behaving in an abusive manner. Or:

2. You are familiar with these games the narcissist plays, and often these false accusations and acts of victimization can lead to extreme cases of confusion and frustration. You can't even comprehend how the "tables are being turned" onto you now. Ultimately, your acts of confusion and frustration which can lead to more arguing and fighting are going to fuel the narcissist even more and significantly drain the energy out of you. Either way, the narcissist wins in this situation.

I hope this list of traits has been eye-opening for you and you have been able to confidently identify a narcissist you may have in your life after reading this list of characteristics. Awareness is the first step. Once you know what you're dealing with, you can begin making the correct choices towards your recovery.

What is the Narcissistic Spectrum?

The narcissistic spectrum is a spectrum of personality disorders that feature zero empathy. These individuals range from narcissistic tendencies to narcissistic personality disorders. At the top end of the spectrum, you will also find sociopathy and psychopathy. These personality disorders all range in the same spectrum because each of them lacks empathy in varying degrees, ranging from difficulties with experiencing empathy to a complete inability to experience empathy. *Some* people on the spectrum can mimic empathy and use this to allow them to blend into society better. These individuals tend to be on the lower end of the spectrum. Others completely lack empathy and are incapable of recognizing it in any degree. They cannot fake empathy. These are sociopaths, and they are generally hazardous people since they can behave in ruthless and violent ways and experience no emotional repercussions from it.

When someone is narcissistic, they may be on the spectrum with narcissistic tendencies, or they may have a full-blown narcissistic personality disorder. Narcissistic tendencies mean that they experience some or most of the traits expressed in the previous section. A full-blown narcissistic personality disorder is seen in individuals who have absolutely no empathy and who suffer every single attribute of the personality disorder, often to a fairly extreme degree.

Chapter 3: The Silent Abuser

Narcissism is known as the "silent abuser" because it tends to creep up on you and you do not notice it until it feels too late to get out. By the time you recognize the abuse, your reality has been distorted, and you have been completely stripped of self-confidence, self-worth, and identity. This results in it being extremely challenging to remove yourself from these situations.

Let's explore what narcissistic abuse is really like and how it actually impacts the victim, particularly in romantic relationships.

A Frog in Boiling Water

The best way to describe narcissistic abuse and why victims tend to remain stuck in the situation is by the "frog in boiling water" analogy. The theory is as follows: if you were to put a frog in boiling water, it would immediately jump out because it knew it was dangerous and it could die. Likewise, if you were to enter a relationship that was obviously abusive from the beginning, you would have left it because you could easily recognize the signs of abuse from the start.

However, if you put a frog in a pot of room-temperature water and slowly increase the temperature over time until it is boiling, the frog will stay in the pot of water until it cooks and dies. This is because the frog never knew when to jump out. It seemed manageable until suddenly it was too hot and the frog could no longer physically get out. Likewise, when you enter a relationship with a narcissist, it is usually incredible in the beginning. There are typically zero signs of abuse. The abuser builds up a persona for you that results in them appearing to be your "one true love." They will do everything to earn your love and make you feel like everything is perfect and you have finally found someone who gets you and who you can settle down with. Then, the abuse slowly starts creeping in. At first, it only happens once in a while. This is how the narcissist can start distorting your reality. They encourage you both to shrug it off as "just a one-time thing." As you begin to agree and shrug it off, they begin to do it more and more. As it increases, your tolerance for their abuse grows. That is until it is eventually so much that you cannot handle it. Before you know it, the abuse is happening daily, and you are justifying it because you have been conditioned to. Because your reality has been distorted, you begin to question yourself. You have been conditioned to accept the abuse and brush it off. Now, like the frog, you are trapped in the boiling water, and it feels almost impossible to leave.

For anyone who is the victim of a narcissistic relationship, this tends to be one of the most challenging parts to accept. Realizing that everything from the earliest moments of your relationship together has been a lie is a tough reality to accept, especially when you are in love. The constant battle between reality and fantasy makes it very hard to leave. Many people are not ready to recognize or admit that this behavior is going on, instead wanting to fight for what they have together because they are afraid of losing the "good" aspects of the relationship. To the narcissist, however, this is all a game. They derive great joy from "hooking" new victims into their abuse cycle, as to them this is part of the joy of a new relationship. For you, it was the intense bursts of love and joy that created the excitement. For the narcissist, it was the sly win that resulted in them coming home with a brand-new prize to abuse and use to fulfill their own selfish needs: you. The narcissist knows that they are creating power over you as time goes on and the more you tolerate their behavior, the more they realize their win is guaranteed. They always start slowly, ensuring that you are not fully aware of what is going on. As your tolerance increases, so do the instances of abuse and wrongdoings. While you are falling in love with them, in spite of their "flaws," they are falling in love with how you are serving them and their dangerous and unhealthy needs.

Signs of Narcissistic Abuse

If you have been abused by a narcissist, you will have symptoms that prove the abuse. These symptoms are challenging. They result in severe psychological trauma to those who have been abused by the narcissist. The signs of narcissistic abuse arise only after the initial love-bombing stops and the narcissist begins their cycle of destroying you. Because it is early on and you are still full of energy and positivity, this part is particularly enjoyable to the narcissist. It also tends to go undetected to you because it starts out slow. They gradually chip away at every positive trait you have, either decimating it or twisting it to be seen as something small, embarrassing, or otherwise unnecessary and pointless. As they scoop these traits out of you, they emphasize all of your bad qualities and press your negativity up, really making it appear like you have nothing positive to give. You only really begin to notice the signs and become aware of this *after* all of your positive traits have been scooped out, and you are left feeling like the worst possible version of yourself. Once you have reached this point, you begin to recognize all of the symptoms of your abuse. At this point, however, it generally feels too late because so much damage has already been done. If you are beginning to reach this point yourself, you may notice the following signs and symptoms arising in your own life.

Using Dissociation as a Survival Mechanism

Individuals who have been abused by a narcissist begin to practice dissociation to protect themselves. Dissociation allows them to detach from their environment, which can disrupt your memory, perceptions, consciousness, and sense of self.

When you experience dissociation, it allows you to numb yourself to the trauma you are facing. You may find yourself using mind-numbing activities, addictions, or obsessions as a strategy to support you in repressing your reality. Often, victims will find themselves slowly becoming more and more addicted to things like video games, scrolling social media, skimming books, cooking, or even taking medications as a way to keep their mind numb to what is happening. Some might even begin experiencing obsessive behavior, finding themselves obsessing over how to maintain their environment "just so" to minimize the abuse and to protect themselves against the dangers of the narcissist. This is how you are able to block out the impact emotionally, so you do not have to feel the pain and the entirety of your circumstances.

This dissociation may also result in you having various parts of your personality that are only experienced and expressed at certain times. You may completely change around certain people or in specific circumstances so that you can support these fragmented versions of who you are. Integrating and reclaiming these disowned pieces of your personality is necessary for you to create a cohesive narrative. This is how you are able to then incorporate your emotional, cognitive and physiological realities together. The best way to seek help on this specific symptom is to receive support from a therapist who is trauma-informed.

Questioning What is Real

One of the primary goals of a narcissist is to suck you into their false reality and isolate you from true reality. This can result in you living a life where the true reality that everyone else is living feels questionable to you. You become confused. Over time, you are conditioned to see the reality the narcissist projects onto you. This reality is one that is self-serving on behalf of the narcissist, causing you to live, breathe, eat, and sleep to their benefit. In this reality that you are sucked into, you are nothing more than a servant of the narcissist's reality. The idea of doing things in a world where everything does not revolve around this person can seem daunting and unlikely. This is because the narcissist has expertly roped you into their world and caused you to divorce your own.

One major symptom that results in you having a dissociation from true reality is memory problems. Many victims of narcissists doubt their own memory and their own view of reality, often relying on the narcissist to feed them what their reality is. This happens because, over the course of the relationship, your very real recollection of events is distorted and twisted by the manipulative narcissist. This can lead to you doubting your own judgment and believing in only what the narcissist says. This happens both as a result of manipulation, sheer energetic exhaustion and a growing inability to fight back. What ends up happening is your own recollection of events and understanding of the world no longer feels valid to you because it has been invalidated and twisted by the narcissist for so long, it can be easy to no longer trust your own perception. The battle of searching between truth and fantasy can be incredibly daunting and exhausting. Becoming so confused and wrapped up in the narcissist's web of lies is traumatizing. You become so confused you don't know what to believe which can make it very difficult to escape the narcissist.

Feeling Like You are Constantly Walking on Egg Shells

Individuals who are being subjected to abuse often feel like they are always walking on eggshells. This is common of people who have experienced trauma in their relationship. It may feel as though you are still afraid of creating a problem, and so you are cautious about what you say and what you do. When it comes to narcissism, in particular, it can be challenging to identify precisely what will set the other person off in some cases. For that reason, your space may feel even more volatile. Certain things may set the narcissist off sometimes but not at other times. This can create even more confusion and frustration within you. You may feel perpetual anxiety looming within you that at any moment you could "provoke" your abuser. This often leads to a fear of confrontation and a lack of boundaries because you do not want to upset the other person.

Sacrificing Yourself to Please the Abuser

If you are the victim of a narcissist, there is a good chance that you regularly find yourself sacrificing your needs, desires, and maybe even your safety to please your abuser. You might recall a time where you had goals, hopes, and dreams and now you no longer work toward these. You might feel like you are alive only to fulfill the needs and agenda of another person and that you are not allowed to or able to satisfy your own needs and desires. At first, it may have seemed like the narcissist's entire world revolved around you. However, over time it will have flipped, and now your whole world might revolve around them.

Everything from your goals, friendships, hobbies, and even personal safety have probably taken a back seat to your need to keep your abuser feeling "satisfied" within your relationship. Though, you will soon begin to realize that there is no way for you to actually ever satisfy your abuser because they are insatiable.

Health Issues and Somatic Symptoms of Your Abuse

Individuals who are being abused, especially by a narcissist, are known to have common health issues and somatic symptoms that are directly related to the abuse. This can include excessive weight gain or weight loss, serious health issues that did not exist prior to the relationship, or physical symptoms that show premature aging. Because of the constant abuse, your body has been under chronic stress and has been producing massive amounts of cortisol. As a result, you begin to have many health challenges.

These health challenges do not simply remain in the physical, either. You may find yourself experiencing anxiety and depression, or even considering self-harm or suicidal ideation. In fact, many people who are subjected to abuse will begin to practice self-harm as a result of the deterioration of their mental health. Another common experience from those being abused is a difficulty sleeping. You may find it challenging to sleep and, when you do, you may find that you have nightmares that wake you. These nightmares are ultimately you reliving the trauma through emotional or visual flashbacks that continually bring you back to the abuse.

The more you remain in the relationship with the narcissist, the worse these stress-related symptoms will become. Because the narcissist is continuously feeding on your energy and emotions to fulfill their own needs, you have nothing left for yourself. Any time you feel any level of positive energy within you, the narcissist will see this energy and take it for themselves, leaving you frustrated and without energy once again. They will continuously push you, striving to get an emotional reaction out of you in any way they can. Through these constant and intense emotional reactions that you are forced into, you grow even more stressed out and wary. Soon, your mental, physical, and emotional well-being are severely compromised, making it even harder for you to fight your way to safety. The stress becomes so high that many victims of the abuse begin to contemplate suicide and other drastic measures of escaping because they are no longer hopeful of a happy life.

You Cannot Trust Other People

Due to the mental abuse you face from the narcissist, you may find that you can no longer trust anyone. Everyone who enters your life may now represent a threat to you in your life. You may become anxious, doubting the intentions of others and assuming for the worst to happen in all scenarios. This becomes even worse because you have experienced the malicious actions of someone who you once trusted but who ended up becoming an abuser toward you. A standard caution turns into hyper-vigilance as you become incredibly aware of anyone and everyone who enters your surroundings and your life.

Because the narcissistic abuser has worked so hard to gaslight you, you no longer believe your experiences are valid. Thus it is a challenge for you to trust anyone including yourself. Even if you feel inside that someone is safe or trustworthy, you may feel as though they are going to hurt you or struggle to actually trust them because of what you experienced in the past.

Self-Isolating Behaviors

The majority of abusers will use isolation as a way to keep their victims away from receiving any help. However, many victims of abuse are also known to isolate themselves. This happens out of shame. Due to the amount of victim-blaming and misconceptions about emotional and psychological violence in society, many victims struggle to trust anyone to support them. In fact, some may be further traumatized by law enforcement, family members, friends, and the friends of the narcissist who may all work toward invalidating the victim's experiences and also promoting the narcissist's behavior. Another common reason why victims will isolate themselves is that they no longer have the energy to deal with anyone else. After having all of their energy sucked up by the narcissist, they do not have what it takes to leave the house, engage with friends or family, or even make a basic phone call to chat with anyone they care about. What small energy the victim has remaining is needed to keep themselves alive and do the very basic self-care acts. Otherwise, they often spend their time quietly tucked away on their own attempting to regain the energy that was stolen from them.

Because the victim lives in fear, believing that no one will understand them, they also fail to reach out for help. Instead, they isolate themselves to protect themselves from further abuse. This is how they relieve themselves of judgment, as well as from experiencing retaliation from the abuser.

You Might Blame Yourself

Narcissists are incredible at shifting blame onto their victim. As a result, you may have been conditioned to take responsibility for their behavior and actions. They may blame you for making them upset, for doing something you knew you "were not supposed to do," and for other reasons. This all results in you feeling like you are responsible for their actions and like you are the problem, not them. It can be a challenge for you to recognize that their behavior and actions is not your fault.

The challenge with this is that it often results in victims protecting their abusers because they do not see them as responsible for the behavior. Due to their conditioning, they begin to look at the abuser as the victim, and they feel like they are the attacker. This creates a challenging complex in their mind that presents an even more significant challenge in allowing the victim to understand the difference between reality and the falsehood they have been conditioned to believe.

You Might Feel Like You are in a Love Triangle

Triangulation is a prevalent tactic from narcissists. They do this by creating love triangles, bringing a third party into the dynamic of the relationship as a way to further terrorize you, the victim. In doing this, your abuser will promote the idea that you are "not good enough," causing you to compete for their attention and approval continually. The person they add to the love triangle can be virtually anyone. On many occasions, this third party can be a friend of yours making things even more dramatic. It could be one of the narcissists work colleagues. You may have slight concerns about this, and they will shame you and guilt-trip you for believing that they would ever do something with another individual.

Part of being stuck in this triangle is that you, as the victim, begin to feel like you have something fundamentally wrong with you. You may start to question why your partner would show more respect and compassion toward someone else than they do toward you. This can lead to you feeling further devalued, resulting in you losing even more self-confidence and self-worth. It occurs in you blaming yourself and attempting to "fix" yourself to please the abuser, who will ultimately never be pleased.

You are Afraid of Being Successful

People who are in a relationship with a narcissist often find themselves afraid of being successful in any way. You know that your abuser has regularly punished you in the past any time you have succeeded. This stems from envy because the narcissist always wants to be the best person around and they do not appreciate when someone else has succeeded and is "outshining" them. The only time that a narcissist will seem to actually be interested in your success is when they can use it as a way to make themselves look better. For example, "My (wife/husband) achieved top rank in (her/his) career this month! I am the person with the best spouse in the room!" This allows them to take responsibility and further increase their own appearance and status as a result of your success.

Many victims find themselves having their success stolen from them as well. If you did succeed, this would mean that you would have something to be happy about that was not directly in relation to the narcissist. They could not take credit for it, nor would your sense of pride and happiness within yourself serve them. So, they steal this away from you as a way to scoop out even more of your self-worth and ability to feel pleasure. That way, you rely solely on the narcissist to be praised and celebrated. You no longer feel safe, capable, or worthy of achieving success anywhere else in your life because the narcissist has manipulated you into believing that the success or praise that you receive elsewhere is shameful and that you should only receive it from them. That way, you remain codependent and stuck in their web.

Still, you might find yourself struggling to even get that far. You may discover that you self-sabotage and refrain from achieving anything in your life for fear of having someone else punish you for your achievements. This lack of moving toward what you love or what you are passionate about often results in depression. Now, you have been isolated from loved ones, perpetually abused by someone you thought you could trust and denied the right to experience joy through the things you love and through success. It makes sense as to why you are suffering so much sadness and depression.

You Lack Self-Esteem and Self-Confidence

Whether you have yet to realize where it is coming from or you have already discovered it, virtually every single victim of narcissistic abuse has severely low self-esteem and self-confidence. This is caused by the abusive tactics of the narcissist. It starts right from the very beginning when they lure you into believing that they are incredible and wholehearted, wholesome people during the initial love-bombing. The very first time the two of you interact, they blitz you into believing that they are a great, genuine person and you fall in love with them.

The more you withstand the relationship and show that you can handle the abuse, the higher your tolerance becomes and the stronger they come down on you. The higher your tolerance for the toxic behavior, the greater the decline in your self-esteem and self-confidence, leading you into a deep and dark place where you no longer have the strength required to fight back and protect yourself. Because your own identity and sense of self-worth are so damaged, the narcissist can easily reel you in again and begin from the very beginning. They will do this over and over again, showing no true remorse or guilt for their actions, and always leading you to believe that you are the problem and that you deserve it. In all reality, you do not deserve it, you never had, and you are certainly not the one to blame. But because you have been in it for so long, you have no way of holding on to any hope that this is true and what the narcissist has told you is a lie to protect themselves and keep you trapped in the cycle.

Your Friends and Family Act Differently

A common tactic used by narcissists is called smear campaigning, which means they tell those close to you many bad things about you behind your back and twist lies to make it seem like you have changed and you are no longer a good person. They do this to manipulate people into seeing you as evil and them as good which further helps their master plan. Keeping you trapped.

As a result of the smear campaigning, you may begin to notice that your friends and family act differently around you or treat you differently from what you are used to. They may stop calling you, address you differently, or even begin to leave you out of various things intentionally. They may also not believe you when you say that you are being abused and that the narcissist has been lying to them. This can make it difficult to get help and ultimately harder to escape.

If you have noticed that your friends and family around you begin to change their behavior toward you and treat you differently, there is a good chance that this behavior is coming directly from the actions of the narcissist. Unfortunately, for many victims, this results in the narcissist having ammunition to reinforce their low self-esteem by pointing out things like "even so and so doesn't want to hang out with you anymore" or otherwise bullying you and using their changed behavior as evidence to why their words are true.

Chapter 4: The Creation of a Narcissist

In this chapter, we are going to explain how narcissistic personality disorder comes to be. This will give you some insight as to how your abuser may have gotten to where they are today. That being said, it is important to understand that most people with a narcissistic personality disorder do not believe they have anything wrong with them. Therefore they very seldom seek treatment. If they do, it will likely not be because you pressured them into it. It is suggested that you use this chapter as an opportunity to understand, rather than as a tool to attempt to show your abuser that they are abusive and to pressure them into seeking treatment.

Causes of Narcissism

The exact cause of narcissistic personality disorder is unknown. Typically, personality disorders are caused by a complex series of issues that lead to the disorder developing. It is hard to predict or determine whether a child will become a narcissist, though there are some things that are believed to contribute to the development of the disorder. Here are the three theories of what goes into the creation of a narcissist.

Theory One: Environment

The first theory involved is their environment. Psychologists and psychotherapists believe that a child's environment can contribute to the potential development of personality disorders, including narcissistic personality disorder. The primary area in the child's environment where these disorders tend to develop is directly in the parent-child relationship. Typically, excessive admiration or excessive criticism toward the child can promote the development of narcissism. If a child is raised by a parent who is a narcissist, they may also learn the behavior and begin to express themselves with narcissistic behavioral patterns. In this case, the person may be on the narcissist spectrum but may not have a full-blown narcissistic personality disorder.

Theory Two: Genetics

As with the majority of illnesses, personality disorders can be inherited by family members. If an individual has one or more people with narcissistic personality disorder in their family, they may be at a higher risk of becoming a narcissist later in their own life. Although this may be an inherited characteristic, there is no way of testing genetics to determine whether or not a person will become or is at risk of becoming a narcissist in their lifetime.

Theory Three: Neurobiology

Neurobiology refers to the connection between the brain, behavior, and thinking. Psychologists, neurologists, and other researchers believe that an individual's neurobiology may encourage them to develop narcissistic personality disorder at some point in their life. Again, there is no way to test a child's neurobiology to determine whether or not they are at risk of developing narcissistic personality disorder in their lifetime. Some theories believe that traumatic life events early in life can change the individuals' neurobiology, thus making them more likely to become a narcissist later in life. This can happen as a result of the trauma itself, or because of the way, their parents may change their behavior toward the child. For example, if the parents' divorce is traumatic to the child and the child becomes neglected by one or both parents. As a result, this can contribute to narcissism. Alternatively, if the child experienced a loss or a personal trauma, such as a serious illness or injury, and one or both parents coddled the child long after the injury attempting to protect them from further dangers, this could also contribute to the potential onset of narcissism later in life.

Risk Factors

Those who are diagnosed with narcissistic personality disorder tend to receive their diagnosis in their teens or early adulthood. That being said, many will not receive a diagnosis because they genuinely believe that there is nothing wrong with them and it is everyone else who has a problem. Despite this being the prime age for diagnosis, some children may begin to show narcissistic traits as they are growing up. Some of these may be typical to their age and will never go on to develop narcissistic personality disorder whereas other children will.

Anyone can be a narcissist, no matter what their age, gender, religion, or ethnic background may be. The disorder is not related to the demographics of the individual so much as one or a combination of the causes listed above.

The general consensus agreed upon by doctors and psychologists is that the biggest risk factor leading to the potential development of narcissism later in life is parenting. Parents who are neglectful, overindulgent, abusive or pathological have a tendency to treat their children in a way that results in the child never actually overcoming the grand sense of self that all children have. In general, children are expected to be more self-indulgent because this is how they learn about their own identity and how they fit into the world. As they grow older, this sense of self-indulgence should fade away over time as they find their answers and begin fitting in. For those who have not been raised in a household where they had access to healthy parenting, either as a result of excessive or neglectful parenting or as a result of constant traumatic abuse, they are at risk of not growing past this self-indulgent behavior. Instead, they use it as a way to feel good in spite of their parents' leading them to believe that they are unworthy of love, or as a way to continue feeling good as a result of their parents leading them to believe that they are special over everyone else and deserve to be treated as such.

Complications

There are many complications that an individual will face if they are diagnosed with narcissistic personality disorder. Of these complications, the majority of them are rooted in social behavior. Individuals with narcissistic personality disorder struggle to maintain relationships, have difficulty at work or school and may resort to drug or alcohol misuse. They are also at a higher risk for physical health problems, depression and anxiety, and suicidal thoughts or behavior. If the narcissistic personality goes untreated, and in many cases even when it is addressed, the individual may experience one or all of these symptoms. This is because, in most cases, narcissists are incapable of admitting and accepting that they are narcissistic. Doing so would result in their entire reality crashing in around them. Furthermore, transitioning from a self-serving lifestyle that others feed into as a result of their abuse and into one that requires them to think of anyone other than themselves is virtually impossible. The amount of pain and loss they would feel from this transition would be more than they are willing to endure. The only time a narcissist may actually seek support is if they have lost literally everyone in their life and they are no longer able to reel people into their abuse cycle. In this case, they may be willing to consider therapy. At that rate, therapy is not guaranteed to be effective as they may just use this as a bargaining chip to confirm that they are "doing better" when, in fact, they are not.

Another major complication that narcissists face lies in shame. As a result of their upbringing and the way they were taught, every single narcissist faces shame in their childhood. Where this shame comes from depends on what caused their narcissism in the first place, but it virtually always results in them feeling the need to "delete" their true self in favor of a false persona, which you will learn more about in Chapter 5. This behavior essentially supports the narcissist in splitting away from the aspects of themselves that they are ashamed of and supports them in creating a mask that they feel should fix what has caused the shame in the first place.

If the narcissist was raised in a neglectful household, the shame would lie within virtually every aspect of the narcissist. As a result, the repeating feeling of shame and neglect would create a sense of trauma in the child that would cause them to want to discard any aspect of themselves that brought them shame or, in their opinion, resulted in them being neglected. Their true self: the parts that they were ashamed of and that they feel lead to the neglect, would then be denied in favor of a false self or mask that would ultimately redesign their profile and make them seem likable to everyone.

If the narcissist was raised in an overly coddled household, the shame would lie within any aspect of the child that was not coddled by the parents. So, if they were deemed an academic genius, anything they struggled with that made them feel as though they were incompetent or uneducated would cause shame. They would become addicted to the praise and the attention they received when they were behaving according to their parents' standards and would feel ashamed about any aspect of themselves that did not live up to what their parents felt was acceptable. This would either be aspects of themselves that contradicted what the parents were proud of, or any aspect of themselves that were ignored or even punished out of them by the parents. The true self, then, would include all of those aspects whereas the false self would seek to discard them in favor of being entirely likable and admirable to their parents.

If the child were abused growing up, any number of aspects of themselves could bring them shame. This can be even further amplified and reinforced if the abuse experienced by the child was also narcissistic abuse. In general, these aspects will directly relate to what they felt caused the abuse. This could lead to a wide range of aspects of themselves that they would then want to discard or decimate in favor of becoming a different variation of themselves that would be void of all of the aspects that they felt lead to their abuse in the first place.

As you can see, there are many complications that can arise in the face of the shame that narcissists feel. Because they blame this part of themselves for the pain and trauma they experienced at various points in their childhood, they feel strongly about the need to hide the true self in favor of the false self, which they feel will earn them greater respect and better treatment from everyone else. Because they embody this false self entirely, this leads to their sense of believing that they are special: because in their eyes, unlike everyone else, they have worked so hard to discard the "bad" parts of who they were.

Prevention and Treatment

Preventing and treating narcissistic personality disorder is challenging since the majority of these individuals will never become properly diagnosed. If the disorder is related to parenting styles, the parent may be unwilling to admit to there being a problem as well, creating further difficulties for the child to get the required care. Still, some preventative measures and treatments are available for narcissistic personality disorder.

If you have a child with this person, you may wish to know how to prevent the disorder from developing in case they have inherited it. The best thing you can do is get treatment for any childhood mental health problems as soon as possible. You can also participate in family therapy as a way to directly support the child, as well as to learn healthy ways to communicate and cope with conflicts and emotional distress in the family. Seeking assistance from parenting classes, therapists, and social workers as needed can also support you in preventing the development of narcissistic personality disorder in your child.

The only true treatment available for narcissistic personality disorder is talk therapy. This psychotherapy strategy supports individuals in recognizing their disorder and can provide them with coping tools that allow them to lead a happier and healthier life overall. This measure does take time, however, and is not always reliable. The narcissist must be fully on board and needs to be willing to completely commit to the process to support the outcome, and even then, results are not guaranteed.

Chapter 5: False-self and True-self

If you recall from previous chapters, narcissists often lure their victims in using a mask. This mask is also called their false-self. The false self is a persona that a narcissist creates that supports them in creating a positive appearance outwardly but does not represent who they truly are inside. While those who have been abused by the narcissist may desire to see their true-self as evil and conniving, the reality is that this true-self is far more complex than that.

In this chapter, we are going to look at the differences between the false-self and the true-self of a narcissist.

The False-self

We regard the "false-self" persona daily in our lives when we look out to society and see our idols, celebrities, and other admirable figures. These individuals all have a persona that they put on for their fans, building their reputation and creating an image that others love to admire. They also have a true-self, the version of self that they share with those who are near and dear to them. The same is somewhat true with narcissists. Except that a narcissist will have a false-self that they show to everyone else and a true-self that only they know.

The false self is a mask that the narcissist creates to design the appearance of being the best. They use this false-self to construct a narrative of their life that is entirely untrue, and they use this narrative to support them in creating their ideal life. A life that is only achieved through deception, abuse, and falsehoods. The purpose of the false-self is to give others the illusion that the narcissist is somehow better than others, that they are living a fantastically grandiose life, often one that is filled with impossible claims. The false-self is constructed in such a way that supports the narcissist in divorcing their true reality and living a delusional life. Any truth that is inconvenient or that takes away from the preferred narrative of the narcissist is denied in favor of their false narrative. A true narcissist will often deny the alternative narrative – the one of the true-self – in favor of the false narrative they have created for themselves.

The narcissist, including all of their codependents, lead their lives by the same narratives. The narcissist uses this narrative to deconstruct and reconstruct the narratives of their victims, bringing them into their falsehood to live in a reality that better serves their desires and needs. Beyond the fact that this narrative is false, the biggest problem is that this narrative does not consider anyone beyond the narcissist themselves. Everyone brought into the narrative is there to serve the narcissists beliefs and views, acting as puppets in his or her storyline.

While many of us will create narratives in our own minds of how things are, this becomes a personality disorder when the narrative is only one person serving themselves through the narratives of many, or when they have become so disconnected from true reality that they become pathological, maladaptive, and dysfunctional.

Once the false-self is formed and functioning, which usually happens in the teen years or early adulthood, it essentially stifles the growth of the true-self and prevents it from operating any further. In other words, the narcissist completely integrates their false-self and completely denies their true-self. In full-blown narcissistic personality disorder, this results in the individual no longer recognizing or understanding the true-self-narrative. In fact, they will often deny that it ever existed in the first place. It appears that these individuals have zero attachment to who they truly are and live entirely in their own falsehood, deceiving themselves and everyone around them to create a life that is less painful than the one that they were originally running away from.

Narcissists often develop the false-self as a way of turning all of their best attributes into who they truly are. This may be because they were excessively admired for these in childhood, or because they were excessively punished for having flaws and so they are trying to discard their flaws entirely. This new version of themselves essentially enables the narcissist to become the person they wish they were, completely denying the person they truly are. This ensures that they no longer identify with the person they were as a child, which they felt was the cause of their parents' behaviors. For example, if a child's parents divorced and they never saw one of their parents after the divorce and felt that they were neglected, they may feel that there was something fundamentally wrong with them. As a result, they would listen for the reasons why other people praise them and begin to obsessively enhance those aspects of their personality while abandoning the aspects that they felt were not as good. This allows them to feel as though they have fundamentally changed who they are so that they are no longer the child who was abandoned for being themselves, even though that is virtually never the reason why a parent would abandon a child.

Another instance that would lead to a child wanting to develop a false-self and live in their mask permanently rather than at the rate which is normal for the average human would be if that child were repeatedly abused throughout their life. The child may then strive to change who they are to discard the aspects of themselves that they felt were responsible for them being abused. They become so good at it that they no longer believe there is anything wrong with them. They literally deny and discard all aspects of themselves that they no longer like; leading them to believe that they are truly the best person ever to have lived.

Not every narcissist will feel the need to change their mask to permanently foster the false-self as a result of attempting to get away from pain or abuse. This is only true for those who have been exposed to abuse or neglect in their childhood. For those who have been raised in an overly indulgent household where the parents coddled the child and never taught them about empathy and always lead the child to believe that they were special, can lead to an addiction. The person essentially becomes addicted to having other people swoon over their best attributes, and so they adapt to believe that they should expect this all their life. When they realize that they do not receive this treatment from others in society, they begin to act with narcissistic behaviors as a way to get it so that they can continue getting their "fix."

For narcissists, the false-self allows them the opportunity to split their personality and choose to permanently live in the narrative of one of the splits. As a result of this personality disorder being pathological, they truly can lead themselves into believing that the alternative narrative does not exist. They may even believe that it never did. This is how they protect themselves from the pain that comes from having aspects of themselves that they were never able to accept or integrate fully.

The false-self has two functions for the narcissist. First, it serves as a decoy. They use it to develop immunity to manipulation, indifference, sadism, exploitation or smothering. So, this is essentially developed by the child as a cloak to protect themselves. The second purpose of the false-self is to use it as a means to barter the way they are treated. They present the false-self as a better self, one that they believe deserves a better, painless, and more considerable treatment by others. It is used to alter others attitudes and behaviors toward the narcissist. So, not only does it protect them, but it also enables them to adjust how other people act toward them to promote a better reality for the narcissist.

Something worth noting is that even healthy individuals will have some level of a false-self. This self is a mask that they use as a persona around the world that they do not know as well. It is typically a more polished, well-created version of self that is shown to others. However, in a healthy individual, this false-self never goes beyond the false-face that they show to those they do not know very well. They continue to have a true-self that they share with family members and close friends who know who they truly are. The only time the false-self becomes a problem is when we use it to suppress who we truly are and ultimately deny entire integration, leading to us splitting off and only leading a false narrative of one aspect of our entire self.

The True-self

The true-self of a person is who they truly are inside. In the case of a narcissist, the true-self does not "die" per se, but it is completely paralyzed and incapable of being expressed by the narcissist.

The best way to understand a narcissist's true-self is to understand that this is typically their inner child. The inner child of the narcissist is often abused in a way that results in them feeling like they are not good enough or worthy enough, or that only certain aspects of themselves are lovable. This leads to the inner child feeling either completely neglected, or specific aspects of who they are being neglected.

If the child is neglected by their parents altogether, they will feel neglected, and therefore their true-self is likely an aspect of them that is filled with feelings of hurt, rejection, neglect and other forms of extremely painful psychological pain. This part of themselves is generally deeply wounded which results in them feeling the need to change who they are entirely by splitting their personality and essentially becoming a new person. By changing away from who they were when they were neglected, the narcissist attempts to become a new "superhuman" type of person who believes that, because their persona is manufactured to be the best of the best, they must be special. This results in them thinking they are better than anyone else, thus leading to the narcissist behaviors. Through this, their true-self – the wounded inner child that feels neglected and rejected – is permanently silenced and they are able to carry on living as though they are better than everyone else and deserve better treatment that results in less pain and more compassion.

If the child was heavily admired by parents, it is likely that the negative aspects of their personality were completely ignored by their parents. As a result, they were taught also to neglect and deny these aspects of self. The child would likely be heavily praised and admired for their positive actions and then would be completely neglected for negative ones. For example, if they scored high on a test, they would be admired, but if they fell off their bike, they would be ignored. This leads the child to believe that they are only worthy of love and acceptance when they are living as their best self. If the less admirable aspects of themselves, which are completely natural to all of us, are too heavily ignored while the other aspects are excessively admired, this can lead to the child believing that these aspects of themselves need to be destroyed so that they no longer experience the pain of having love or acceptance withheld.

Either way, the true-self is often highly damaged and wounded in a narcissist. They choose to deny it because, in their eyes, the true-self is responsible for attracting all of the pain and trauma unto the child. By denying this aspect of themselves and essentially destroying it and replacing it with the false-self, the narcissist can become the person that they feel is worthy of a higher degree of admiration, appreciation, acceptance, and love by others. Unfortunately, the creation and integration of the false-self lead to them not only protecting themselves from the pain of their own abuse but also results in them abusing other people in an entirely different way later in life.

The form of abuse that this leads to them casing unto others rarely looks like that which they learned in childhood unless their narcissism was a learned trait after being raised by a narcissist. The difference here is that the narcissist will generally abuse people on the pretense that they are not as good as the narcissist is and therefore they should be ashamed of themselves. Because the true self of the narcissist was never accepted and they felt it lead to so much pain, many times the narcissist grows deep, unrealized jealousy over those who live their lives genuinely *feeling* worthy as their true selves. They tend to feel angry that they were raised in a way that denied their true self when others seem to live just fine with it. As a result, they take this anger out through their abuse, destroying others' in the ways that they felt they were destroyed. In other words, because they felt that they were not allowed to be accepted for their true self, they feel that no one else should be, either.

Chapter 6: A Narcissist's Target

Narcissists, like all abusers, have a preferred "victim" that they will go after. These victims are individuals who are most likely to assimilate into the narcissists narrative, allowing them to continue to create their own false reality. If you are in a relationship with a narcissist, you may be wondering just what initially got you into this position.

"Why me?" is a massive question that victims will ask. You may be feeling like the narcissist chose you because there is something inherently wrong with you. Alternatively, you may be feeling like there is something wrong with you because you were unable to predict the abuse and so you begin to feel ashamed in yourself. Trust that you becoming the victim is not your fault. It is not because there is anything wrong with you at all. Instead, the narcissist may have simply realized that you are highly empathetic, compassionate, and caring, and used this to exploit you into becoming another person in their falsehood reality.

Still, there are certain traits and features that all victims tend to have in common, at least to some degree. The following characteristics are the most common traits seen on the resume of a narcissists target.

Conscientiousness

One of the most overlooked qualities that a narcissists victim will portray is conscientiousness. Narcissists know that if an individual is conscientious, they are more likely to follow through on their commitments and will typically assume that the narcissist will do the same. As a result, they are able to exploit this quality to have the victim serve *them* directly.

A person who is conscientious tends to give other people the benefit of the doubt. They are more likely to grant second chances and become admissive of the narcissist's behaviors. Because this individual is already willing to give extra chances and see the good in the narcissist, the narcissist knows that they can exploit this behavior to turn a conscientious person into a pushover with an excessive need to please. If you are excessively agreeable and conscientious, you have the perfect characteristics required for a narcissist to groom you to fit their needs. They will take advantage of you, repeatedly abusing you and destroying you as you continue to choose to see the best in them. Because of your desire and need to see the good in others, you are less likely to see the narcissist for who they truly are. They thrive on this dynamic because it means that not only are you not seeing them for who they truly are, you are not even looking for it. You would rather see the good in them and give them the benefit of the doubt than admit to yourself or anyone else that they are acting out of any other reason than love or misguided attempts at showing love.

Empathy

Having empathic tendencies is a necessity if you are going to be chosen by a narcissist. They love seeing empathy in their victims because this means that you are probably extremely easy for them to manipulate. To them, this is your greatest weakness, and it will become their greatest weapon against you. Since a narcissist craves and needs attention, praise, and affirmation from others, they prey on individuals who have a high degree of empathy. These individuals are far more likely to provide the attention they need so that they can feel good.

As an empathetic person, you are more likely to be able to relate to how the other person is feeling and, as a result, you act according to what you are feeling and not necessarily what you are seeing. For a narcissist, this is a perfect dynamic. Because they are feeling a significant amount of pain and torture deep inside, they know that you can sense this and that you will take pity on them. Then, they twist that pity to get what they need out of you. They also use your empathetic side to devalue you, knowing that you are led by emotions. Those who are led by emotions tend to be easier to manipulate as all the narcissist has to do is play on your emotions by creating a sense of shame, guilt, and disappointment within you. Once they have done that, they can control when you get to feel good and when you don't.

Another great aspect of you being empathetic means that you will listen to their sob stories and feel for them. They will lie and manipulate you into believing that they are the victim, validate why, and trust that you will feel for them and that you will want to save them from being the victim. They know that you are more likely to forgive because you want to see the good in others. This only further reinforces their belief that you are not able to "think" for yourself, thus allowing the narcissist to hijack you through your emotions and force your perception to fit their needs.

If you are a highly sensitive empathetic person, often referred to as an Empath, this means that you are driven by your emotions more than the average person. Not only can you relate to what the other person is feeling, but you can genuinely feel it, too. This means that you are even more likely to take whatever they tell you and give them what they desire because you genuinely want to help them *feel* good. Only, they never will because they truly can't. As an Empath, you may be even more at risk for narcissistic abuse because of your very nature. You have a plethora of the one thing the narcissist lacks most: empathy. They flock to you like moths to a flame.

If you believe you are an Empath and want to learn more about what this means and how you can protect yourself, you can refer to my book: *"Highly Sensitive Empaths: The Complete Survival Guide to Self-Discovery, Protection from Narcissists and Energy Vampires, and Developing the Empath Gift."*

Integrity

A morally impoverished narcissist is extremely drawn to someone who is impeccable with their word. If you have integrity, you have many attributes that a narcissist can exploit for their own personal gain. Many people who have strong integrity will not cheat on their moral code or give up on a relationship. It is easier for the narcissist to keep them trapped in the relationship until they are no longer capable of leaving because of the psychological damage that has been caused.

Narcissists feel no remorse for harming their victims. However, their victims will often feel morally apprehensive about retaliating in any way. The victim, with strong integrity, does not want to betray the relationship or step back from the obligations they feel they have to the narcissist. This integrity can benefit the individual who is in a relationship with other like-minded individuals, but to one who is in a relationship with a narcissist, it can keep them trapped for years.

Resilience

An individual who is resilient is capable of enduring tough situations. The narcissist exploits the resilience of the victim in order to strengthen the bond between the victim and the abuser. This may seem counterintuitive, but it actually serves the narcissist in a big way. Individuals who are incapable of enduring the abuse are more likely to leave their relationship quite early. Those who can "toughen out" the abuse, are more likely to stay within the relationship because they heal in between incidents and can, or so they think, handle them as they happen. If the victim does leave the relationship after realizing how abusive or toxic it is, an individual with a high resiliency will bounce back during their time apart. During the hoover phase (described in detail in Chapter 7), most victims will return hoping that things will be better. If things are not better, the victim knows within that they have the strength to endure the abuse.

Resilience is a powerful quality to have that can deeply support you in overcoming adversity and achieving anything you desire in life. However, when it has been twisted around the desires of the narcissist, it can become a painful weapon that strengthens your ties to your abuser and makes you less likely to leave the relationship. A person who is resilient may be more likely to ignore their instincts to leave, choosing instead to stay and fight it out. They may adopt one of two mentalities: that of a fighter, or that of a savior. Regardless of which mentality the victim adopts, it is regularly used to attempt to sustain an unsustainable relationship.

Due to the trauma bond that the victim develops with the toxic narcissist, the victim may find themselves measuring their love by the amount of cruelty that they are willing to put up with. Sentences like "you constantly lie to me and yet I am still here, how is that not a measure of love?" may cross your mind or your lips in arguments if you are an individual with great resilience, caught in the terrifying relationship between the narcissistic abuser and victim.

Weak Boundaries

Individuals with already weakened boundaries are admirable to the narcissist because this means that they are easier to take advantage of and keep in their web. People who are strong in their boundaries will strong-arm the narcissist, blocking them from having the capacity to abuse them and leaving when they realize the relationship is toxic. However, those with weak boundaries already struggle to stop people from mistreating them. This means that they already have some tolerance built up for abuse, making it easier for the narcissist to pull them into the abuse cycle and keep them trapped.

If you are someone who struggles to enforce boundaries or does not recognize what healthy boundaries look like, this makes you an admirable target for the narcissist. This is even further enhanced if your weak boundaries are in direct relation to how you allow people to talk to you and treat you. If you allow people to exploit you, take advantage of you, and treat you poorly because you are unsure as to how to stop it or already feel weak against them, this means that you are already a prime candidate for abuse. Having weak boundaries can also tie in with next trait we are going to talk about; co-dependency.

Co-Dependent

Many people do not realize that they are already codependent. However, if you are already co-dependent, a narcissist will recognize this quickly and use it to their advantage. The narcissist's entire objective is to create a victim that is entirely dependent on them for virtually everything. If you are already conditioned to be codependent, this means that they do not have to condition you and it makes their job easy. Instead, they simply have to encourage you to attach yourself to them (or their web). The hardest part of their cycle is already done, making it even easier for them to hook you.

The typical tell-tale signs of codependency that narcissists will look for in potential victims include the victim messaging them first majority of the time, asking to hang-out most of the time, feeling the need to share more than seems natural for early on in a relationship, and seeking for validation and approval from the narcissist. This needy, and overly-invested behavior means that you are likely co-dependent, which makes you an easy target. The narcissist will not have to put in much work to make you become even more invested in the relationship. This also makes it easier for the narcissist to keep you stuck in their web and keep using you as narcissistic supply.

Sensitive or Passionate Romantic

People who identify as sensitive or as passionate romantics are preferred by the narcissist. These individuals are easily swooned by the love-bombing phase, which helps the narcissist hook them in and keep them invested in the relationship. Because very few people are as intensely romantic as the passionate romantic identifies as, and even fewer are perfectly curated for the individual, this makes them easier targets. The narcissist can easily look into what makes you feel loved, how they can romance you, and what it would take to sweep you off your feet. Then, they tailor the love-bombing phase to you. Through this ability to curate the perfect love-filled scenario for you, the narcissist is easily able to hook you in.

Because you are a sensitive individual, this also means that you take heartbreak and pain harder than the average person. The narcissist is aware of this and knows that it will be even harder for you to leave them compared to the average individual. As long as they make the pain of leaving more than you can bear to endure, they can feel confident that you will not be going anywhere any time soon. And as a result, they gain even more power over you and can keep using you as narcissistic supply.

Sentimentality

Another thing that narcissists prefer in individuals is a high degree of sentimentality. People who are more likely to love deeply are more likely to bond quickly and deeply with the narcissist, making their abuser-victim relationship strong. Narcissists will generally love-bomb their victim, appealing to their desire to have a strong and deep relationship with their lover. This is how they lure them in during the early stages of the relationship. This enables the narcissist to secure the love, trust, and commitment of the individual early on.

The narcissist will exploit the individual's sentimentality to create pleasurable memories that the victim will romanticize and hold onto during periods where the abuse takes place. This encourages them to see the good in the narcissist, resulting in them being more likely to forgive their abuse and see it as a bad day or a mistake.

Once the individual has committed and is deeply in love with the narcissist, the narcissist will begin to withhold emotions and withdraw as a way to create feelings of emotional depletion in their victim. Then, the victim begins to scramble to hold on and make things "better." They are more likely to rationalize and justify the behavior, omit it from punishment, and protect the abuser if the victim is first filled with love and positive memories to hold onto.

The Recipe of the Perfect Target

An individual who possesses all or most of the traits listed above is a perfect target for a narcissist to latch onto and exploit for their own sick games. These characteristics all work together to design an individual who is susceptible to being abused and staying in the cycle. They are more likely to forgive and move past the abuse, they are easier to form deep bonds with, and they are capable of continuing to love the narcissist and fulfill their need for love, attention, acceptance, and praise.

If you possess these traits, there is a good chance that they were exploited to being used against you. Sadly, most of these traits are positive traits for any individual to carry. When they are used in a healthy setting, they support you in leading a highly connected, successful, thriving life that can have positive outcomes. When exploited by an abuser, however, they can quickly become weapons that are used against you.

Instead of creating a positive connection they are used to design a forced connection with the narcissist. Instead of encouraging success, they are used to devalue you and prevent you from creating any level of achievement in your life. Instead of providing you with the ability to thrive, they are used to suck the life out of you. Narcissists are highly powerful at using your best traits and characteristics to turn them into your worst nightmares. This is what makes them so powerful. They are sneaky about it, and they will play you in all of the right ways to keep you hooked and coming back for more.

Please, do not let this information dishearten you in any way. Remember, awareness is the first step to escaping the narcissist and beginning your road to recovery.

Chapter 7: The Abuse Cycle

The narcissistic abuse cycle is somewhat straightforward, but also extremely complex. While writing it out on paper is fairly easy, the execution of it is challenging. Being on the victim side is even more difficult as you are regularly blindsided by the cycle, often to the point that you do not see it happening at all. It may take many experiences of the cycle, maybe even years of being trapped in it before you actually see what is happening. Even then, it often goes on for a long time before the victim is finally able to walk away for good.

Being able to recognize and leave the abuse cycle is extremely challenging for a victim because they are constantly battling between emotions and logic, reality and fantasy. Emotions are what hook them in, to begin with: the deep passion, the intense feelings, and the love for the narcissist. However, as they begin to see the narcissist's mask slip from time to time, their logical mind begins to kick in. This can lead to you doubting the validity of your emotions and wondering if it is all just a lie, or if your emotions are telling the truth. However, because they are so strong and intoxicating from the narcissist's abuse, most victims who begin to hear the voice of logic will just as quickly silence it in favor of their addiction to the moments of praise and pleasure they receive from the love-bombing phase with the narcissist.

Many times, victims know that the narcissist is abusive or toxic because their logical mind can identify it. As a result of their emotions, however, the victim doubts this reality and keeps themselves entrapped in the relationship by following their heart and avoiding pain, rather than seeing the situation for what it truly is and finding safety outside of it. Especially if the victim has high traits of co-dependency, the alternative option of leaving can seem just as painful, leaving the victim in a catch-22 or in other words, stuck.

This chapter is going to give us the opportunity to explore the abuse cycle itself in an in-depth manner, as well as the different styles of abuse that are employed by the narcissist to create the desired effect. This will support you in recognizing how it happens, as well as understanding the specific tools that your abuser is using to facilitate the abuse.

Outline of the Abuse-Cycle

Before we get into detail on the cycle itself, you must know the outline. I also want you to know that reading this may be challenging if you are just beginning to realize that you are in a relationship with a narcissist. If that is the case, take your time and go easy on yourself. You have already begun the healing process.

The outline of the cycle of abuse that victims experience by their narcissist contains 5 phases. These 5 phases are:

- Idealization
- Devaluation
- Discarding
- Destroying
- and Hoovering

The Abuse Cycle

The following five steps are all a part of the narcissistic cycle of abuse. These happen in virtually every single cycle, so it is important to be cautious and aware. If you are a victim, pay attention to these cycles so that you can begin to witness them as they happen. This will support you in having a greater understanding of your abuser, seeing the reality behind what they are doing and giving you the power to leave.

Idealize

The process of idealizing allows the narcissist to make themselves appear better than what they really are. During this stage, they often do what we call love-bombing. This means that the narcissist starts creating an ideal relationship for you by showing you massive amounts of interest, love, and affection. This leads to you developing a deep sense of trust toward the narcissist, helping you to connect with them on a deeper level. Or, so you think. You share many things with them, letting them know about your deepest secrets, hopes, and fears. They share information with you, too, though it is rarely genuine. In many cases, it may not even be the truth.

The narcissist will continue to string you on for a while, making the relationship seem almost too-good-to-be-true, but never letting the other shoe drop. At least, not until it is the right time to do so. Instead, they let you grow deeply comfortable with them. They give you enough time to develop strong feelings for them and to see what a great person they are. Or, what a great person they want you to *think* they are. The connection and ecstasy shared between you two is simply amazing. You can't believe you have met someone you can connect with on a deeper level mixed with explosive physical chemistry. You can't get enough.

For the narcissist, this phase is all about collecting data. Everything you are sharing with them is being stored away to be later used against you during the phase of devaluation. They want to create a secure environment for you so that you feel like they have everything you want, and they want to know everything about you, so they can use it against you in the future. Once they've got you hooked, they know that you will do anything to protect the relationship. For the narcissist, this is the key step for them being able to keep you attached to them for as long as possible.

Devalue

Once the narcissist is confident they have hooked you significantly, and you are heavily invested in the relationship, the narcissist will then start to move into the devaluation phase. This is where they begin to chip away at you and shift your perception so that your strengths now appear as flaws. The process of switching from idealization to devaluation is slow. At first, you won't even recognize it because it is so subtle. They intentionally bring it out very carefully, increasing your tolerance for their abuse as they go along. They may start out with all pull and no push, reeling you in and keeping you coming back for more. Over time, however, this begins to change. Soon, there will be 10% push, then 20%, then 30% and so on and so forth until the entire relationship is filled with majority abuse and toxicity. The gradual increase takes months, even years to reach maximum capacity. The length of time it can take and the amount of pressure put on the victim all depend on the signals you are giving off and your level of tolerance. The narcissist wants to know that they are winning, and they want to feel confident that you are giving up. If you have stronger boundaries going into the relationship or you demand that the relationship starts at an even 50:50 for power and control, they will continue to apply the amount of pressure that you can handle without recognizing what is going on until they win.

At that point, however, you are the frog in boiling water. They have conditioned you by building up your tolerance over a long period of time, and you didn't even see it coming because of how gradually it happened. If the narcissist was to do it any other way, you would see the abuse and leave. So, they strategically measure out only what you can handle and continue pushing more and more. They may have to throw you a bone every so often and give you some pull in the form of flattery or affection. The main goal is to shift the ratio to majority negativity and build up your level of tolerance, chipping away at your self-worth more and more. As your level of tolerance towards the abuse grows, it becomes harder for you to leave.

Once the narcissist feels that they have reached a high enough push/pull ratio, they know they have reached a state of control. Here, they feel powerful over the relationship, and they begin to get worse and worse. They begin to take advantage of the fact that they are now in control and the pressure becomes even greater, perhaps causing the ratio to increase far quicker now that they know you will not leave. During this part of the process, they will also be targeting other potential victims to attempt to lure them in. This way, when they reach the devaluation phase with you, they can begin getting attention from someone else. This keeps them in the constant state of receiving attention, yet perfectly grooming everyone else to give it to them.

The devaluation phase of the process is very painful and traumatic to the victim. If you were once known to be confident and sexy, they would now push you into believing that you are actually cocky and vain. If you were once intelligent, you are now a know-it-all. They use the devaluation phase to gaslight you, invalidating your feelings and beliefs and abusing you into believing an alternate reality that is far from the truth. Here, you begin to have your self-image, and self-worthiness cut down. Your successes begin to mean nothing as they discourage you and fill you with doubt, fear, and insecurity. They use the devaluation phase to prevent you from creating future success, as well as to create deep insecurity that causes you to feel like you are incapable of escaping. This part of the abuse cycle can be highly traumatizing as the narcissist will seek to destroy you in every way possible.

During the devaluation phase, the majority of victims have no idea what they are actually experiencing. They do not know what they are going through. Victims are entangled in a web that is spun by the narcissist and, often, they have no idea that they are even in it. It is extremely painful when in this stage. The heart-breaking thing is the victim will do everything to fight to get back to the initial love-bombing phase of affection, chemistry, connection, ecstasy, and love. But it is too late. This is exactly where the narcissist wants you.

From here, the narcissist will do one of two things. If they are not yet certain about where you stand and how deep you are in the hole, they will move back and forth between the idealization and devaluation phase. Each time, the devaluation phase will grow longer and longer, until eventually, you are here almost permanently. At that point, you will only be entered into the idealization phase as rewards for your behavior if they feel that you deserve it. That way, they continue to give you small reasons to stay with them, which you will cling to as a result of your internal emotional and mental destruction. This enforces your codependency on them and allows them to slowly but consistently hack into your self-confidence, self-esteem, and self-worth. At this point, you are still desperately clinging onto the initial love-bombing phase and the idea of leaving the relationship is more painful than tolerating the abuse. Once they are confident that you are officially hooked and that they can treat you in any way they want, they will begin including the discard phase.

Discard

During your desperate attempts to get back to the initial phase that felt so good, the narcissist will discard you. Because you are now feeling deeply insecure and insignificant, they know that you will do anything to seek their approval. This essentially conditions you to seek excessive admiration from the narcissist, putting the power directly in their hands. Now, they use your need for validation to support their own agenda. They will frequently withdraw, telling you that everything you have done for them is a sign of failure, and blaming you for not making them feel "good." That way, you begin to blame yourself. As you continue to seek validation desperately, they use all of your attempts as a way to feed and fuel their own need for validation, attention, praise, and admiration. In other words, you are feeding the fire.

This behavior supports the narcissist in scooping out all of the remaining qualities within you that do not serve their agenda. At this point, they know that you are so desperate for their attention and affection that you will do nearly anything to win it back. So, they scoop away. They know that there is a good chance that you have not even yet begun to realize how minimal your self-esteem and self-worth has gotten because the devaluation has been so slow and gradual. To them, this means that you are oblivious to what is keeping you attached, which means there is little chance that you can or will break the attachment. You may grow frustrated and leave for some time, but this rarely lasts. You would first have to recognize what was going on and then receive help to leave the situation permanently, which is an unlikely scenario for most victims.

At this point, nothing you can do will fill their high standards. They set their standards higher and higher, continually putting them out of reach so that you cannot possibly achieve them. As the blame shifting continues, they will use your desperation and confusion as an opportunity to turn themselves into the victim. Often, they will blame you for stuff that they have done themselves and then delude you into believing that it was you who actually did it.

As this is all happening, the narcissist will be bringing other people into the dynamic. During your time apart, they will bond with other victims to fill their needs and create a love-bombing phase. In their mind, they are creating back-up plans of narcissistic supply just in case you do manage to escape forever. The narcissist cannot cope alone. When you get back together with the narcissist, they will claim that this person is close to them but that it has no impact on your relationship. They will then successfully keep two or more of you trapped in this cycle, constantly switching between which one has the "pleasure" of filling their needs. The narcissist will rarely if ever, spend any time alone during these discard phases. Even being alone for as little as a few nights is plenty enough time for triangulation to root in deeply and start, especially because the narcissist has already been priming their next victim since the devaluation in most phases.

In some cases, victims will leave the narcissist first. Rather than waiting for the discard phase to begin, they take the cue and choose to leave on their own. This can happen in some cases because they do not understand why the narcissist is treating them so poorly and they are struggling to find any reason to stay. So, the victim threatens to leave. If the victim does not leave, this will only further anchor in the narcissist's attempts to devalue their victim. If the victim does leave, they will not be gone long before the hoover phase starts. Through the hoover phase, the narcissist harasses the victim until they willingly give the narcissist attention once again. Then, the idealization phase starts once more so that the narcissist can re-hook the victim and bring them back into the cycle. The more the hoover phase is successful, and the victim is lured back, the stronger the hook grows and the harder it is for the victim to endure the discard phase when it inevitably arises once more.

Destroy

At this point, there is a strong possibility that the relationships the narcissist has been working on behind the scenes with other victims have now become more developed. The narcissist now has more sources of narcissistic supply and is less dependent on you. This is where the destroy phase starts to begin.

During the destroy phase, the narcissist will continue to pressure you into taking the blame. They will then dig deeper into a devaluation process, using your weakness and vulnerability as an opportunity to really drive their abuse deep. They will often switch back and forth between the two phases, making you feel worthless and causing it to seem like if you leave you will have nowhere to go and no one to turn to because you are not worthy of anyone's care or love. They will also make it seem like you have no other choice but to leave because you are no longer welcomed to stay with them.

Here, they will use all of your insecurities against you. Everything they learned about you during the idealization phase will come back to haunt you as they twist it deep, causing you to doubt yourself and to see your strengths as your biggest flaws, leaving you to feel like you have nothing left to offer. If they know that you are afraid of being seen as needy, for example, they will use your desperate attempts to seek validation as a way to amplify this insecurity and peg you as excessively needy. They will exploit all of your insecurities, fears, and elements of your past to cause you to feel completely unworthy.

Here, you begin to believe them. Your spirit is crushed, your hope is destroyed. You begin to feel as though they are your only cure and you *need* them to undo what they have done. For that reason, you continue to try to seek their validation and do everything that you can to have them accept you and "make everything better." Now, you no longer have the strength to walk away, nor do you feel like you can undo the world of hurt and pain they have caused within you. You seek to them as your remedy, though you may also begin to withdraw for fear of being lashed out at and hurt again. You are likely left in this uncomfortable phase of needing their validation but feeling too hurt to talk to them or seek it any further. You are destroyed. Your energy is depleted, and you no longer have what it takes to continue fighting. To the narcissist, you are like a tired prey who have ended their running and is ready to roll over and admit defeat.

During the destroy phase, the narcissist will go to any great length to ensure that you feel completely unworthy and unwanted. They will say things like "No wonder your mother doesn't like having you over anymore" or "This is why your friends don't hang out with you anymore" to make you feel like you have nowhere left to turn. In reality, the narcissist is the direct reason why these individuals no longer see you as often.

Other things the narcissist may say during the discard phase include things like: "I never loved you," "I can't believe you thought I would care about you," "Your boyfriend from the eleventh grade was right, you are fat and worthless," or anything else they can draw on to make you feel like you have nothing. They want to take everything away from you, leaving you feeling like you are stranded on an island. Because they back everything up with painful evidence from your life, stuff that you have confided in them previously, they can easily manipulate your emotions to leave you feeling like they are right. Now, the only thing left for you to do is beg for forgiveness for something you never did or leave and attempt to regain everything you lost.

Hoover

Once the destroy phase is over, you and the narcissist will most likely spend some time away from each other. You may have escaped yourself or the narcissist may have temporarily abandoned you. If you are coming out of the destroy phase for the first time, you can be sure it is not over. While the narcissist will have their other victims beginning their abuse-cycle phase, you will be put into the hoovering phase. The narcissist likes to have back-up plans.

The hoover phase is actually where the majority of the trauma will occur, despite the rest of the cycle being exhausting and traumatic as well. Here, victims typically cannot fight their addiction or need for validation. Some might escape for a few weeks or even months, but most will return in the end. No matter how hard they try, their life always seems to feel empty without the narcissist because they are no longer being used and abused in the way that they have been conditioned to. The narcissist has expertly conditioned them into needing this abusive situation, making them eager to come back to the narcissist for more. Despite it being a long time, the victim also still will endlessly crave the initial idealization phase. That is unless they have adequate support in leaving the situation and are able to seek assistance in staying away.

Soon, the victim begins to idealize the relationship in their own mind. They miss the narcissist, so they begin ignoring all of the bad and negative experiences in favor of the ones that brought them joy. They romanticize the idealization phase and minimize the rest. After enough time passes, the narcissist knows that the victim will begin downplaying the abuse or even going so far as to believe that it was barely abusive, to begin with. Many times, they will think if they were to do things differently, then the relationship would have been better. This leads to them longing to have the relationship back.

In the meantime, the victim finds it to be quite challenging to assimilate in the normal world. Their independence is challenging to get back, they rarely have any confidence, and it is challenging for them to get into any further relationships because they simply do not feel as though are good enough for anyone else and able to trust anyone. The words of the narcissist ring through their minds, reminding them to feel that they are not worthy of the love or affection of anyone. As a result of the abuse and the destruction of their self-esteem and self-confidence, the victim will now also likely begin experiencing self-sabotaging behaviors that further minimize their sense of self-worth. These behaviors will not necessarily be related to dating or relationships, either. Some self-sabotaging behaviors that are common in victims during the hoover phase include things like overeating, sleeping too frequently, giving up on exercise, not engaging in social activities or anything else that keeps them from re-entering normal life as they knew it before the narcissist. The victim will often find themselves feeling lonely and unhappy, and they begin to feel like they need the narcissist back just to defeat the loneliness. They may begin to idealize again in their own minds, which leads them back to the narcissist where it starts all over in the idealization phase.

During this phase, the narcissist will also regularly make attempts to reconnect with the victim. These attempts will most likely be made when they are not receiving attention anywhere else, thus resulting in them needing a fix. Chances are, they are connecting with other victims at the same time, seeing who will fill their needs first and in the most effective way possible. The messages will often start with a simple "Hey" sent to the victim's phone or inbox. Then, it will move on to messages that are used to lead the victim into believing that the narcissist sees what they have done wrong and that they will not do it again. Small attempts of love-bombing and idealization will occur. For example, messaging the victim a text like "Hey cutie, how are you? I miss you terribly."

Through the conversations, the narcissist sets the belief that they will be better again and that this relationship will be the way it was during the idealization phase. This plays into the victim's hope that things could be better if they were to act differently and certain things were changed this time around. The narcissist plays on this belief, leading the victim to feeling confident that it would be better if they were to try again. This, however, is untrue. The narcissist has no intention of being kind or compassionate, however. Instead, they will remain the abuser, and the victim will remain the victim. What is actually happening here is a power dynamic, where the narcissist is luring their victim back and getting an ego boost by knowing that they can go back to their "old supply." This is essential for you as the victim to understand: the narcissist *will not be any different.* Even if they revisit the idealization phase to bring you back, they are still abusive, and they will still devalue, discard, and destroy you. This is likely to happen several times over and over again, sometimes tens or even dozens of times before the victim ever understands what is going on. In some cases, the victim never will, and they will live out their entire life being lured back and forth by the abuse of the narcissist. Eventually, it happens so often that the narcissist barely even makes an attempt to hide themselves or their intentions anymore. They are so confident that you will come back that they simply wait for you to come back on your own, or they make futile attempts to lure you back in if they feel you do not come back quickly enough.

If you do not give in to the attempts of the narcissist when they begin trying to reconnect, they will often begin attempting to punish you as a way to lure you back. They will start using smear campaigns, lying to those in your life or anyone who will listen to them to lead them into believing that you are a bad person or that you are someone who they shouldn't associate with anymore. These smear campaigns are often done in an effort to isolate you, pushing you to feel lonely so that you will message them back. They know that if you have no one and they approach you with a promise of love and affection that you are more likely to respond to them. So, they will do anything it takes to get you into that state that will surely leave you wanting to come back to them. In their eyes, they want you to behave as they have trained you to even when you are no longer together. In your eyes, you have nowhere else to turn.

Cycle Symptoms for the Victim

The previous steps were the abuse cycle that you will experience step-by-step with the narcissist. However, there is also a victim cycle. This cycle is perpetuated by the abuse and is the cycle that the abuser wants you to become trapped in. They want you to continually move back and forth between these two stages: cognitive dissonance and codependency. That is how they keep you weak and returning for more.

Cognitive Dissonance

The first stage of the cycle for the victim is cognitive dissonance. Cognitive dissonance is the mental pain and discomfort experienced when a new contradictory belief clashes with an original belief, by some new evidence. After being under a false belief about someone for quite some time and then having that belief gradually peeled away as they expose who they truly are, can be excruciatingly painful. Not only is it painful, but it is also immensely overwhelming and very hard to accept as a new reality. Especially when there is so much emotion attached to the original belief.

In healthy scenarios, cognitive dissonance is an opportunity to learn more about ourselves and correct our beliefs and behaviors. In unhealthy scenarios, such as with abuse, cognitive dissonance can be far too painful for the victim, that you refuse to change your beliefs despite witnessing new evidence. Even though logic may serve in showing that your original beliefs and emotions towards the narcissists were incorrect, it is very difficult to override your original beliefs because of the sheer pain and tragedy that would arise from this experience. For many, it is too much to bear and keeps the victim trapped in the narcissist's web.

This battle of cognitive dissonance within the mind of the victim can go on for months or even years. As the abuse from the narcissists continues to grow, and their mask gradually slips bit by bit, the victim receives more and more new evidence contrary to their original beliefs about the narcissist. As difficult as it is, the victim needs to detach from their original beliefs about the narcissist in order to free themselves.

Co-dependency

Once the narcissist has given the victim a glimpse of their true-self behind the mask in the de-value phase, the victim will fight to get back to the idealize phase. When this occurs, the narcissist will use this to their advantage and drive you into a state of co-dependency. This is the part of the greater cycle where you begin to desperately seek validation and affection, and they proceed to the discard and destroy phases. Because they are in the power position here, they can pressure you into feeling like you are incapable of doing anything and you *need* them to support you in becoming capable. The narcissistic abuser wants you to feel like they are your lifeline and you are unable to achieve, do, or be anything without them. This is how they ensure that you are going to come back for more.

When you are abused into a state of co-dependency, it can feel like you are unable to step away on your own. They have you exactly where they want you at this point. You feel incomplete, and they are the "missing piece," and so you will always come back for more. Co-dependency as a result of abuse is a psychological disorder that is rooted deeper every time the cycle is completed, and you are scrambling for their validation and acceptance. Unraveling it and realizing that you are capable of being whole and independent on your own is a challenging process that, in most cases, requires a professional support system to help you untangle yourself from the web.

You can often tell you are co-dependent by looking for one key change in your behavior: where your needs lie. If you feel that you need the other person to make you feel happy, like you have nothing without them, or like you require their validation to make decisions in your life, there is a good chance that you are experiencing co-dependency.

If you are experiencing co-dependency in your relationship, it is important that you take the measures to heal this through therapy following the termination of the relationship with the narcissist. Co-dependency can carry on into other relationships going forward, often sabotaging otherwise healthy relationships or worse: lead you directly to another narcissist. Getting proper help can support you in making sure this does not carry on and that you are not further harmed by the narcissist going forward.

Feeling Guilty

A state that is often felt by the victim of abuse is a deep feeling of guilt. When the narcissist manipulates you, they lead you to believe that you are the one in the wrong. They use evidence from your time spent together and from your past to validate why you are the attacker and why they are the victim. You are manipulated into feeling guilty for supposedly hurting them. You may even find yourself taking responsibility for the downfall of the relationship, feeling like it was your fault that you had a falling out and the narcissist never did anything wrong. If you do still see the wrongdoings that they have done, you will likely justify them by believing that they were only done in response to what you had initially done to them.

The reality is that you never actually did anything to earn the abuse, nor did you even instigate the falling out in the first place. Instead, this is another symptom of the narcissist successfully abusing you and manipulating you into seeing them as the one who needs attention and care. This way, they do not have to admit to doing anything wrong, nor do they have any reason to apologize. You, however, feel like you must do far more than what is reasonable to receive their forgiveness. This is where they get plenty of attention to fill the needs that they felt were not being met, which likely caused them to instigate the initial arguments in the first place.

Fear of Being Alone

Many victims find themselves fearing loneliness. Because you have been repeatedly told that you are worthless and no one would ever love you, you quickly find yourself fearing loneliness. This happens in two ways.

In the bigger picture, you are afraid of being left by yourself and never finding love again. So, you cling to your relationship with the narcissist to avoid an extremely lonely fate. The narcissist purposefully instills this phase, knowing that this will decrease your chances of escaping.

In your day-to-day life, this may even manifest as a fear of being alone even for a short period of time. You may feel like whenever you are alone, you could easily be abandoned or neglected. You may also begin to sit with your thoughts and realize how toxic the relationship is and then begin feeling immense pain for these realizations. Alternatively, you may sit by yourself with the intense fear that the narcissist is cheating on you or spending time with one of the people whom they have brought in for the purpose of triangulation, rather than doing what they have actually said they are doing.

Fear of The Truth

While some victims of narcissism will be hungry for the truth, others may actually fear knowing it. This ties in with the battle of cognitive dissonance we mentioned earlier. Although the facts may be clearly there, it can be easier for the victim to 'turn a blind eye' and cling to their original beliefs during the love-bombing phase. Learning the truth could affirm many painful pieces of information to the victim that can lead to deep feelings of embarrassment, heartbreak, and shame.

For example, perhaps learning the truth confirms that they have indeed let someone else lie to them, exploit them, and abuse them for however long the relationship with the narcissist lasted. Perhaps learning the truth confirms that the narcissist has been cheating on the victim for however long. This can be painful to admit that you would allow such a thing to happen in your life. In reality, the victim has only allowed it to happen because they had no idea that it was actively happening.

It is important to note, that after a lot of time and pain has passed, some victims will no longer want to avoid the truth. Some will actively seek out the truth despite how painful it may be, especially following the end of the relationship. There comes a point where knowing the truth helps the victim understand the reality of the relationship and can support them in escaping the narcissist and staying away. The more they know, the more evidence they have that the relationship is toxic and will not change and therefore it gives them even more reason to believe that the relationship will continue to be painful and harmful.

Chapter 8: Escaping and Healing

Escaping and healing from a narcissistic relationship is one of the most challenging things that we can do. There are many things emotionally and psychologically that keep us trapped in the relationship. Some victims may fear being physically abused by the narcissist as well. Having the ability to break the trauma bond, safely escape, regain your independence and heal the trauma is essential but challenging.

Breaking the Trauma Bond

One of the biggest reasons why it is such a challenge to escape from a relationship with a narcissist is because the victim forms a trauma bond with the narcissist. Trauma bonding is a form of strong emotional attachment that an abused person forms between his or her abuser. It is perpetuated by the cycle of abuse and reinforced each time the abuse-cycle is successfully completed. While bonding in and of itself is natural and healthy under the right circumstances, bonds developed in the process of abuse are unhealthy and traumatic to the victim. People who have grown up in abusive households are more likely to develop these bonds with multiple people because, to them, this is a "normal" bond to have.

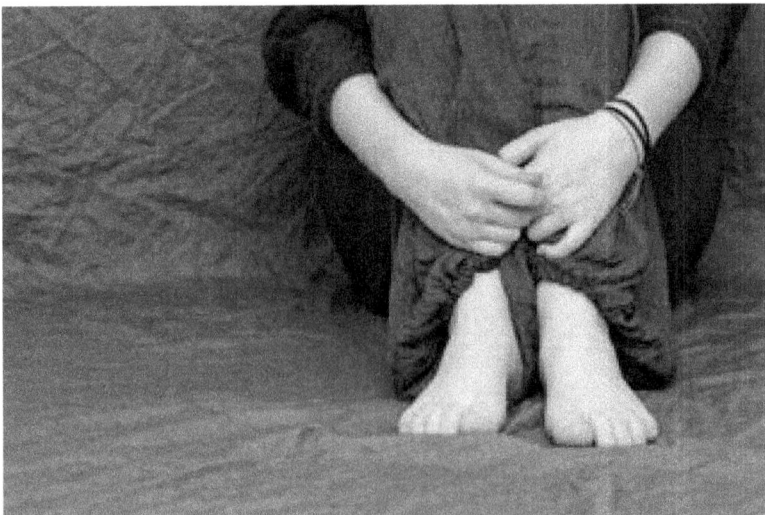

In addition to the trauma bond itself, there is also damage that occurs within the brain when we are exposed to abuse for a long period of time. When you have been abused, you will likely suffer from some degree of Complex Post-Traumatic Stress Disorder (CPTSD). CPTSD is a psychological condition that is stored in various places throughout the brain, making it challenging to release and eliminate. This disorder will actually rewire your brain, causing you to chronically live in a state of fight or flight. While you can still resume a relatively normal life following the breaking of the relationship and abuse cycles, if CPTSD is not properly healed you will carry it with you for life. Because it will rewire your brain, you will essentially train yourself to live around the symptoms of CPTSD, which can result in you losing your quality of life and feeling like you are trapped even long after the break.

Breaking the trauma bond is an essential part of leaving your abusive relationship. It can be a challenge, but it is possible. The first step is to consciously decide that you want to live in reality and not within the falsehood of the abuse. It starts with confronting all of the denials and illusions that you have lived in, including the ones the abuser made for you and the ones you made for yourself. It is essential that you realize that this person is abusive and will never change. Of course, it is okay to grieve this as it truly does feel like a real loss. You are losing a person whom you thought you had, but you never truly did.

In addition to choosing to consciously live in reality, you need to create boundaries. There should be a no-contact boundary between you and your abuser. You do not contact them, ever. If for some reason you must keep them around, such as if you share custody of children, minimize the contact and keep it very focused on necessary topics and nothing else. Breaking your habits and changing these patterns can be a challenge, but they are necessary. It can be extremely helpful to seek external support to assist you in relieving yourself from the trauma bond, and other aspects of trauma that linger in your brain. Healing does take time and having professional support is extremely beneficial for your long-term health. Be sure always to choose a therapist who is trauma-informed, so they genuinely understand what you are going through and what you need.

You should also understand that breaking trauma bonds takes time. Be gentle and patient with yourself. Remember, the creation of the bond itself was not overnight. It took time to build so it will take time to unravel and eliminate as well. Stay intentional and focused but be patient with yourself and all of the challenges that you may face in the process.

Escaping Safely

The very first thing you absolutely must know before leaving a relationship with a narcissist is that they *will* continue to try and manipulate you. They will pressure you into believing that you are overreacting, blame you for everything that happened, and attempt to con you into believing that they genuinely miss you and that they want you back. An abuser will always make false promises of a better future to draw their victims back in. It is essential to understand that you cannot trust anything they say, ever. Anything they attempt to do is in an effort to manipulate you back into the relationship. You must try to look at the bigger picture and understand the narcissists end goal. It may take you a few rounds of the entire abuse-cycle before you finally realize.

It is also essential that you leave cold turkey and allow yourself to endure the pain that comes with it. You may feel as though you are unable to, but trust that you can. Again, seeking support from understanding loved ones and trained therapists can be incredibly helpful at this point. Instead of contacting the narcissist in a moment of weakness, contact a loved one or a professional instead.

The Extreme Importance of No Contact

To successfully escape and stay away from the narcissist, you *must* enforce 'No-Contact.' If you feel that you are in serious danger from this person, having a legally enforced law surrounding the No-Contact order may be required to ensure that you have the support of law enforcement in this clause.

If you have any contact with the narcissist whatsoever, you are giving them easy access to manipulate you and keep you in the relationship longer. No matter what you think, this will be true. Any time you communicate with the narcissist, every single piece of communication will be designed to manipulate you and lure you back in. If you communicate with the narcissist, you are allowing your own mind to justify and rationalize why it may be a good idea to go back to the narcissist. You have to realize you are in a very vulnerable and weak position at this moment of time. You must vanish from the narcissist and focus on your recovery. You have to refrain from contacting them for any reason whatsoever, unless it is absolutely mandatory (such as if you share children with them.) And even if you do share children, you must work towards creating an understood schedule between both parties, where no communication (or very minimal) is needed.

Whenever the narcissist begins the hoover phase and starts trying to lure you back in, you must also understand that they are doing so only because they are lonely and they want to exploit you for their own needs. There is nothing genuine here. They do not miss you, love you, or need you in their life no matter what they say. This can be extremely challenging to understand and to embrace on an emotional level, especially because of how you have been abused and lead on by the narcissist. Because of the number of emotions that may arise any time you feel the need to contact them, or anytime they contact you, having a trauma-informed therapist and empathetic friends or family members that you can turn to during these times will be extremely supportive in helping you stay away from the narcissist.

Realize that no matter how good your intentions are in leaving the relationship, you will have to fight temptation. It is very easy for your mind to replay the good times from the relationship and to convince yourself that things may be different the next time you go back. Many victims will leave the relationship with no intention to go back, only to be lured back in *dozens* of times before hopefully realizing that things will never change. This is because you have a trauma bond, which keeps you seeing the "good" in this person and justifying your return. What you are actually seeing are the lies and manipulation, but as a victim, it can be extremely challenging to decipher the difference. This is because it would require you to admit and endure the reality that *every* aspect of the relationship was a self-serving lie fed to you by the narcissist. Which, understandably, is extremely challenging for anyone to admit, let alone endure the aftermath of the admission. This aspect can lead to complex PTSD, that makes it mentally devastating for any victim to attempt to endure or leave.

Another reason why your No-Contact order is absolutely necessary is that the hoover and idealization phases are so well-refined with a narcissist, and you are already so mentally destroyed from the CPTSD and trauma bond, that there is virtually no other way to overcome this aspect than to seek professional support and break contact. As a victim, you have become addicted to the idealization phase. What leads you back and causes you to justify the rekindling of the relationship is generally the fact that you desperately want to have that deep, passionate, tailor-made love once again. It is something that is rare to find in organic relationships, thus meaning that you have likely never experienced anything like it. It gives your mind a high with the hormones of dopamine and serotonin that actually physically leaves you addicted to this phase. You become so addicted to it that, like anyone addicted to anything else, you easily overlook the dangerous and damaging parts of the addiction in favor of your "fix." This only further supports the narcissist's hoover phase, which ultimately leads to a relapse every single time.

When leaving the relationship with a narcissist, ensure your physical safety and maintain *absolutely no-contact*. I cannot stress this enough. During this time, you will be extremely vulnerable to "relapse" into the addictions of the relationship and the only way that you can completely avoid this is by quitting the relationship cold turkey and never looking back.

Healing from Your Narcissistic Relationship

The healing process is not fixed within any particular time frame. How long it takes varies from one person to the next. There are many things that you can do to promote healing, however. The following practices will help you hugely with healing yourself and healing the trauma within your brain. It is important to understand that healing trauma in your brain is a lengthy and challenging process and that it is best not to do it alone. Seeking support is always the answer, and it is also essential to make sure that the support is empathetic, caring, and genuinely invested in your healing. You are vulnerable at this time, so be cautious not to jump into another abusive situation when seeking support.

Having boundaries is essential. You should begin practicing boundaries with yourself and with other people around you. When you have been abused by a narcissist, boundaries are something you have been conditioned to eliminate so that you can be fully available to the abuser. It is time to start practicing saying no and being very choosy about who you let into your life. Be picky with the energy that you let into your life.

You need to spend some time eliminating the toxicity from your life. Since you have been very isolated during this experience, externalizing can be helpful. Practice journaling, speaking your truth, and talking to a trusted loved one. Getting out everything you have been holding in can be very therapeutic in helping you release everything built up inside of you and moving on.

After a long time of lies, it is essential that you take this time, to be honest with yourself. As well, you need to forgive yourself. Realizing that part of you knew and forgiving yourself for knowing but not feeling strong enough to do anything about it is essential. You should also forgive yourself for anything you hold against yourself regarding your relationship. Trust that if you could have done better, you would have done better. Abuse can be tricky, and you are the victim, not the abuser.

Doing the deep work is important. When we are abused, we carry a lot of damage within us. This is where you are going to get to work through your inner trauma and heal everything inside of you. Spend time going through the pieces of you that feel broken and addressing them one by one. This is where having your therapist on board can be helpful, they can listen and provide you with professional support when addressing the particularly painful parts that you have been holding on to. You can also use other practices, such as yoga or spirituality, to draw you into yourself and help you explore the parts of yourself that have been hurt and hidden for a long time.

Shifting your focus is another essential part of healing from abuse. You need to make sure that you are engaging in your reality and focusing on the world around you. Be patient with yourself and practice engaging bit by bit. This is a good time to practice rebuilding your independence, going out on your own and with loved ones without the abuser, and being your true-self. The parts of you that were dormant for so long can now be appreciated and adored again. Ask people how they are doing, get involved in the lives of the ones you love, and begin integrating yourself with the world around you again.

It is time to start bathing in self-love again.

Chapter 9: Healing Your Sense of Self

In Chapter 8 we discovered the importance of various healing strategies that would protect you from the physical and neurological aspects of your abuse. However, there are many psychological aspects that you are going to need to heal as well. Being able to reintegrate into society after having been a victim of narcissistic abuse is extremely challenging. As a result of your abuse, many aspects of your life have become casualties. You have more than likely lost many friends and family members, hobbies and passions, your sense of self-worth and self-image, your self-respect, and other important aspects of your life. If you truly want to heal all the way from your narcissistic relationship and the damage you have endured, you need to focus on healing these aspects of your life as well. In this chapter, we are going to explore how you can do just that.

Restoring Your Sense of Self

After an abusive relationship, losing your sense of identity is an extremely common, yet extremely damaging side-effect. This is exactly what results in victims staying in abusive relationships for so long, and why relapses occur. The victim simply does not recognize themselves outside of the relationship anymore. Rebuilding your sense of self after leaving your narcissistic relationship is a vital step in healing yourself so that you can begin living again. This is how you can begin to remember who you are, rebuild your confidence, self-respect and self-esteem, and feel worthy of being a part of society once more.

The first step to doing this is to focus on remembering that you are worthy. It can take some time to rebuild your sense of self-worth. You can begin healing your sense of self-worth by affirming it to yourself on a regular basis. In the mirror each morning, focus on affirming your worth to yourself. Affirmations like "I am worthy," "I deserve to be happy and healthy," and "I deserve to be respected" are great affirmations to begin building your sense of self-worth. You can also begin affirming yourself any time you make decisions. If you do not feel comfortable affirming in front of the mirror, you can write down positive affirmations that resonate with you in a journal. Or you can listen to a positive affirmation's audiobook. Whatever you are comfortable with. Creating these affirmations for yourself is a powerful way of personally reminding yourself that you do, in fact, deserve to be happy, healthy, respected, and loved. This will slowly begin to unwire all that was built-up on the contrary by your abuser.

Next, you need to begin rebuilding your support team. Being able to feel worthy and deserving of a great life will require you to have those feelings reinforced by others. Here, you are not looking for someone else to affirm to you what you cannot affirm in yourself. That would be a byproduct of codependency as opposed to a healthy support system. Instead, look for supportive people who can help you affirm these things to yourself. People who are willing to help you see this in yourself can support you in remembering during your more challenging times that you deserve to heal and have a better life. You want to surround yourself with good energy and a supportive environment.

You can also begin building your confidence by building your knowledge. One of the first ways that you should do this when you are healing from an abusive relationship is to begin building your knowledge in the abuse that you endured (in this case, narcissistic abuse,) and the symptoms you have as a result. Understanding this can empower you to see where you were lured in and how it was not your fault. It can also help you feel more confident in refraining from being trapped in another similar situation in the future. When you can begin to identify and understand the warning signs, it becomes a lot easier to feel confident in your own ability to protect yourself and support yourself in having better experiences in the future when you are ready.

Lastly, make sure that you spend time getting to know your *own* warning signs and symptoms. Pay attention to what it feels like to dislike something and how it feels to choose in your favor. Begin listening to your inner voice again and trusting in it. After the abuse, trusting yourself on even the most basic things can be a challenge. Letting yourself remember what this voice sounds like and trusting in it, is a big way of giving your power back to yourself so that you can become your own advocate once again.

Spending Time Doing What You Love

For as long as you have been in the relationship with the narcissist, you have likely never been allowed to have time to engage in doing what you love. If you did, it was likely heavily conditioned and controlled by your narcissistic partner. As a result, you may feel many emotions of shame, guilt, and uncertainty around doing the things that you love doing. However, it is essential that you begin. Giving yourself the time to build up to doing what you love again can support you in feeling worthy, but it can also support you in having greater confidence in actually engaging in these activities.

When you first start doing what you love again, you may feel many emotions arise within you. Of these emotions might include deep feelings of unworthiness that result in you feeling like you no longer want to engage in these activities anymore. It is important that you address where these emotions are coming from. If you feel like you personally do not want to do these activities anymore, there may be a good chance that it is because of the trauma bond and your CPTSD. To see if this is genuinely your own dislike or as a result of your conditioning, commit to doing the things that you used to love doing for a set amount of time and ensure that you continue going for the entire duration that you decided early on. Then, at the end of that period, revisit your commitment. If you decide you still do not like doing that activity anymore see if you can replace it with a new one.

If you find that you are struggling to derive any joy at all from any of the activities you try, make sure that you bring this up with your therapist. One big symptom of CPTSD derived from abuse is depression, which can result in you feeling like nothing brings you joy anymore. In this case, there may be alternative solutions to help you overcome this sadness so that you can get back to doing the things you love.

Do not feel the need to do everything you love all at once. Take your time and start with just two things. One can be bigger, like an activity or hobby that you love, and one can be smaller, like indulging in the tea that you love or adding a small element back into the daily routine that brings you joy. Having these two easy commitments to start off with will give you time to settle back into doing things you love without feeling overwhelmed. Then, as you begin to feel more confident and comfortable with these activities, you can add in more until you are doing all of the things you love once again. If you ever begin to feel overwhelmed with what is on your plate, know that you are in control and you are allowed to slow down and adjust as needed. Stay focused and clear on what your needs are and make sure that you continue to address them as you go. When you were in the abusive relationship, your needs were rarely met or addressed. For that reason, overlooking them can lead to anxiety and stress. However, having more attention on them than you are used to can do the same. Taking it easy and letting yourself have space and time needed to readjust is important.

Focusing on Your Exercise and Diet

When we are under a certain amount of stress in our lives, the first things we tend to overlook are our exercise needs and our diets. Neglecting these is a sign that you are under a lot of stress, but they are also common when we stop addressing our own needs in favor of another person's, such as in an abusive relationship. When you are reintegrating after a significant relationship that was ridden with abuse, it is important that you place emphasis on your exercise needs and your diet. Getting the right amount of nutrition and exercise can do you a world of wonders in supporting your body and mind in having the proper nutrients to lift it out of chronic stress and alleviate the symptoms that come with chronic stress.

For your exercise needs, it is a good idea to consider joining some form of exercise class or a group with others who will exercise with you. This can support you in staying dedicated, as well as support you in relearning how to socialize outside of your abusive relationship. Creating new friendships, contacts, and individuals can be refreshing. These individuals do not know your ex-partner, so they are not likely to have any idea of what your ex-partner may be spreading about you through smear campaigns. Additionally, they do not know you as an "abused person," meaning that you are free to just be *you* around them. This freedom, alongside a healthy new exercise regimen, can be very helpful to anyone who is coming back from an abusive relationship.

You should also make sure that you are eating properly. Those in abusive relationships have a tendency to either under eat or overeat due to stress. Depending on which you struggle with, you will need to choose a healthy diet plan to help you eat a healthy, balanced diet that is appropriate for your needs.

There are also some nutrients that you can use to help you with your mood when you are healing from the mental and emotional side effects of abuse. Vitamins B and D, niacin, and omega fatty acids are all known to help promote greater brain health and elevate moods. Adding these to your diet can support you in having better health overall so that you can begin enjoying your healing process and finding more joy in your day to day life.

Rebuilding Relationships That You Lost

Over the course of an abusive relationship, many other relationships are lost. As a way to prevent you from being able to see the capacity of what you are trapped in, and to avoid you leaving, abusers will always do their best to isolate you from anyone you were previously close with. Furthermore, the shame, embarrassment, trauma bond, co-dependency, and CPTSD you experience as a result of your abusive relationship can lead to you isolating yourself as well. This means that over even a relatively short period of time with a narcissist you can lose a lot of relationships with members of your family and your friends.

As you heal from the narcissistic relationship, rebuilding these relationships is important. Each of these relationships represents something you lost during the relationship with the narcissistic partner, so healing them can help you heal in general. However, going about healing these relationships may be uncomfortable or even difficult. Knowing how to repair something that has been so deeply damaged can be a struggle for people who are already going through so much as a result of the aftermath of an abusive relationship. For each relationship you want to repair, you may find that you feel embarrassed to approach the individual. If you isolated yourself from the relationship, you might feel guilty for doing so and worry that they will not forgive you. It is important to understand that in most cases, they will. If they don't, it is simply because they do not understand. Having a therapist to speak with as you rebuild these relationships can support you in navigating the relationship either way.

When you go into rebuilding these relationships, it is important that you are open and honest about the abuse you endured and how it impacted your life. You might worry that people will not believe you or that they will blame you for not knowing sooner and doing better. In some cases, this may happen. However, most people are actually understanding and empathetic toward these situations and will be willing to both listen to you and forgive you for the loss of contact for however long you experienced it.

After you have been open and honest, begin making an effort to communicate with these individuals on a regular basis. Rebuilding the relationship will take time and practice, so be patient and do not expect them to all get better at once. A great way to go about this part of the rebuilding is to set a goal to communicate with one person outside of your household on a daily basis. This way, you can begin rebuilding these relationships steadily but not in such a way that it becomes overwhelming and depletes your already low energy.

Ultimately, it is important for you to start hanging around positive and encouraging people for your health and well-being. This will help your mind to stop replaying all the events that occurred with the narcissist and also help in preventing a relapse. It is time to start focusing on you and your life now.

Starting A New Hobby

Hobbies are a wonderful way to support your healing journey. They are great for distracting you from what you have experienced, offering you a boost of confidence by giving you a sense of understanding and knowledge over something you enjoy, connect you with other people who share the same hobby and support you in networking, and promote a sense of happiness and joy within you. There are many positive benefits to having a hobby that you can enjoy in your life.

The key when healing from an abusive relationship that encouraged self-isolation is to choose a hobby that is going to support you in getting together with other people. If you enjoy something that tends to be more solitary, such as reading, consider joining a book club that will allow you to get together with others and begin socializing in a normal setting again. This way, you can do your hobby on your own time but also gain the valuable benefits of socializing out of it.

The hobbies that you choose to get into once again can be new or ones that you loved previously. There is no limit on which you can choose or how many. This is a great time to practice listening to your inner desires and needs and doing something you love. Choosing something that you are interested in and that will bring you great joy is a wonderful way to remind yourself that you are worthy of having joy and love in your life and that happiness is something you deserve to experience. This could include playing a musical instrument you have always wanted to learn how to play, or perhaps taking up a new sport or maybe learning to speak a new language. This is a great way to practice self-love and begin adding things back into your life that makes you happy. It is also a great way to open yourself up to new possible opportunities.

As with the other practices, when you are just starting your healing journey, focus on picking something that will be more manageable for you. Attempting to do too much at once or trying to get right back to where you were before the abusive relationship can be overwhelming and intimidating. When you realize that you are not the same person that you were before the relationship and that your ability to do things the way you once did have changed, you may actually end up feeling worse off. Starting off smaller and slower can support you in easing back into being a person with confidence, high self-esteem, and self-respect. Set manageable and reasonable goals for yourself, celebrate yourself each time you achieve them, then move on to the next one. This will make your healing journey much easier.

Physical Healing Practices

There are many powerful physical healing practices that you can begin incorporating into your regular life that can support you in healing from abuse. Acupuncture, eye movement desensitization and reprocessing, yoga, reiki, shaman work, energy healing, and even hypnosis can be powerful in helping individuals who are healing from the aftermath of abusive relationships.

Acupuncture helps by supporting energy in moving through meridians in the body, helping to release blockages and eliminate stress build-ups. When healing from an abusive relationship, this can support you in letting go of things that you have been subconsciously holding onto for the duration of the relationship. It can also promote healing by supporting you in moving through the natural energies and emotions that come with your experience.

Eye movement desensitization and reprocessing is a practice that some therapists use that have individuals move their eyes in a specific way when recalling memories. This movement is believed to support the brain in becoming desensitized to the neural pathways that are integrated with the trauma of the abuse. It also supports you in creating new neural pathways that are healthier and that bring less stress into your body and mind.

Yoga is another wonderful exercise-based practice that you can use that supports healing. This is a form of exercise, but it emphasizes intentional movement and the processing of energy and emotions. When used regularly, it can support you in having a healthier response to stress stimuli which can support you in healing from the chronic stress you accumulate when you are in a toxic relationship with someone who is abusive, such as a narcissist.

Reiki and other energy healing practices can be powerful in supporting individuals in healing from narcissistic relationships. These practices are believed to promote the movement of energy in a way that is similar to acupuncture, but that does not use needles or, in many cases, physical touch in any way to promote this flow. Having Reiki or any other energy healing incorporated into your healing can be a great way to support you in feeling better on an emotional level.

Hypnosis is another type of healing, sometimes associated with energy healing, that can support you in releasing trauma. When you work alongside a professionally trained hypnotherapist, they can tailor hypnosis sessions specifically for your needs. These sessions are designed to promote the reprogramming of new neural pathways in your brain to support healthier responses to stimuli in your environment.

Using any number of these healing strategies is a great way to support your healing overall. You can also mix them together to increase your healing capacity. The best way to discover which will work best for you is to begin practicing each one and see which feels best. Incorporate the ones that feel best into your regular healing practices. While these will not replace the support of a high-quality trauma-informed therapist and a support team, they will add to your healing and help you to heal in a whole way. Approaching your healing with a mind-body-spirit approach can ensure that you release any remnants of the trauma so that you can restore your entire self.

Crystals That Support Healing

In addition to using energy healing practices as mentioned in the previous section, there are many crystals you can add to your healing practices. Crystal therapy is believed to support individuals by adding vibrational frequencies into your energy field that promote healing. You can incorporate crystal therapy into your daily life by purchasing crystals that you can wear, hold, or keep nearby.

The following crystals are known to be great for promoting healing:
- *Rhodonite* is a crystal that is associated with the heart and is believed to support individuals in healing from a broken heart
- *Obsidian* is known to expel negative energies from your body, mind, and environment
- *Jade* is known to support you in calming your emotions and overcoming stress

- *Amethyst* can protect your energy field from psychic attacks while also supporting you in overcoming addictions (such as the ones you have to the narcissist's "idealization" phase,) as well as to overcome depression related to your trauma
- *Banded Agate* is believed to protect you from intrusive memories, which can support you in refraining from going back to the "good" times with the narcissist
- *Sugilite* which can support you in overcoming stress related to your trauma
- *Citrine* which can help you repair your negative self-image
- *Selenite* which can help you overcome the anger associated with your trauma
- *Rose Quartz* which can promote gentle healing of the heart and bring calming love back into your life

Start Traveling

Traveling is one of the greatest things you can do for your healing and your road to recovery. While you may not want to start traveling right away, once you begin feeling better you should embark on at least one traveling journey. Traveling on your own can be a powerful way to rebuild your self-confidence and self-esteem, refresh your mind, add new experiences and practice becoming independent so that you can begin breaking your co-dependency and engage in some genuine self-care.

Many people who have survived abuse find that even when they are away from their abusive relationship, their environment is filled with memories. You may find frequent places that you went to with the narcissist, such as shopping malls, grocery stores, or other places, which bring up memories. Leaving this behind, even if only for a short period of time, can liberate you from these memories and help you gain perspective.

Plus, traveling independently gives you free time to be with yourself, remember who you are, and begin learning how to love yourself once more. You can discover how you feel best supported, what acts of self-love make you feel best, what you like to do when you are alone, and what you don't like to do. These intimate pieces of information that you gain about yourself build your self-confidence by giving you the opportunity to know yourself in a deeper way than you have for some time.

Before you embark on traveling alone, make sure that you are safe from the hoovering narcissist. Do your absolute best to make sure the narcissist does not find about your travel plans. Make sure they are blocked on your mobile-phone and blocked on every social media platform. That way, your experience remains positive, and you can focus completely on your healing and recovery.

Chapter 10: Terminology Index

Here is a list of some terminology that you may not fully understand or know the meaning of:

Accuse
When the narcissist accuses other people of engaging in destructive or abusive behaviors, such as lying, manipulating, rather than admitting that they were to blame.

Cognitive Dissonance
When it comes to psychology, cognitive dissonance means you are in mental discomfort due to holding two or more contradictory values, beliefs, or ideas. In this case, it is from trying to hold two contradictory realities together in your mind: the true reality, and the narcissistic falsehood reality.

Conditioning
The process of psychologically training or altering someone so that they behave in a desired manner.

Devaluation
The phase in the abuse cycle where your abuser attempts to reduce or eliminate your worth and importance.

Discard
The phase in the abuse cycle where your abuser attempts to discard you by withdrawing and psychologically pressuring you into a desperate attempt of "winning them back."

Gaslighting
An abuse tool where abusers invalidate the victim, manipulating them into questioning their own sanity.

Hoovering
The phase in the abuse cycle where your abuser attempts to "suck" you back in through luring you to re-engage in your relationship with them.

Love Bombing/Grooming/Idealization
When a narcissist creates a mask, appearing to be the perfect "Prince Charming" for you. Here, they put you on a pedestal and give you everything you ever wanted so that you have the illusion that you are perfect together.

Triangulation
When a narcissist brings a third party into the dynamic of your relationship to use against you. The third person is awarded attention, affection, and respect while you are neglected and abused.

Narcissistic Supply
The people who have already been abused by the narcissist and are more likely to come back. These are people who are most vulnerable to being readmitted into the abuse cycle with the narcissist, feeding their needs. A narcissist regularly keeps a few on hand in case they are not being fueled elsewhere.

Projection
When an individual project's their beliefs, values, opinions, emotions, actions, or behaviors onto another person. In a narcissistic relationship, this is where the abuser would blame the victim for something that was actually done by the abuser.

Smear Campaign
When an abuser discredits you to friends, family, and anyone who may be capable of supporting or assisting you behind your back. This is how they gain power by eliminating your validation and credibility and leading others to believe the narcissist over you.

Stonewalling
When a narcissist or abuser becomes evasive and begins blocking or delaying you. They will regularly give vague or evasive answers to questions or simply ignore you until they feel like stopping.

Reality Distortion

When an individual alters another's reality for their own personal gain. For the narcissist, they alter their victims sense of reality through evil tactics such as compulsive lying, manipulation, and victimization.

Victimization

When someone turns themselves into the victim, even though they are not necessarily the victim of the circumstances. In narcissistic relationships, this is a manipulation tactic used by the narcissist to cause the victim to feel as though the narcissist is the true victim, thus causing the narcissist's victim to feel guilty and remorseful. In this case, the victim was never in the wrong, to begin with, but the narcissist has expertly flipped the switch and caused them to feel like they were.

Final Words

Thank you for reading *"Emotional and Narcissistic Abuse: The Complete Survival Guide to Understanding Narcissism, Escaping the Narcissist in a Toxic Relationship Forever, and Your Road to Recovery."*

I recognize that based on the nature of this book, it can be a challenging one to read. You may be facing many emotions after reading it, so I hope you have been seeking support or finding ways to allow yourself to integrate this information so that you can use it to support your escape and healing processes.

If you have already left the narcissistic relationship, I commend you. I know that is a very challenging process and you have done a wonderful thing. If you are struggling, be sure to reach out for help and continue reaching until you are pulled out. I know this can be an extremely challenging time. Do not beat yourself up over it. Trust that this is not your fault and that you are absolutely not to blame for any of this, no matter what anyone may try and tell you. There is a happily ever after for you.

The next step is to carry on in healing from the breaking or now-broken bond between you and your abuser. Continue working in the direction of healing as much as you can, taking it one step at a time and always focusing on the outcome. Trust that you have an outcome on the way and that it will not always be like this.

It is natural to feel stuck or unable to do this on your own. That is because healing from abuse is a painful process that often requires professional support and a lot of time and effort put into healing. Please do make sure that you reach out. I know that until now you have been conditioned to isolate yourself. This should be the first thing you start undoing by reaching out and receiving support from others. Keep trying until you get it; you can do this. Even if it has been some time since you left and you are feeling stuck, reach out. There is no time frame for healing. Do what you need to do. Be kind and be patient with yourself.

It is important to note that many people who experience narcissistic abuse during a toxic relationship with a narcissist are likely to be particularly sensitive and can easily feel the emotions and feelings of others. If this sounds like you, there is a good chance you are an Empath. If you don't know what an Empath is or you are curious to find out more, be sure to check out my other book *"Highly Sensitive Empaths: The Complete Survival Guide to Self-Discovery, Protection from Narcissists and Energy Vampires, and Developing the Empath Gift. "*. In it, you can learn more about what being an Empath means, how it impacts you, why narcissists are drawn to you, and how you can protect yourself on a deeper, energetic level.

Lastly, if you found this in any way helpful to you, please take the time to review it on Amazon. Your honest feedback would be greatly appreciated and it will greatly help many other lost souls out there who may be struggling and in a time of need.

Thank you.